D0193165

TEACHING IN CIRCLES

TEACHING IN CIRCLES

My Journeys in Teaching
High School

NATHAN R. MILLER

KAPLAN

PUBLISHING

New York

© 2009 Nathan R. Miller

Published by Kaplan Publishing, a division of Kaplan, Inc.
1 Liberty Plaza, 24th Floor
New York, NY 10006

All rights reserved. The text of this publication, or any part thereof, may not be reproduced in any manner whatsoever without written permission from the publisher.

Printed in the United States of America

Library of Congress Cataloging-in-Publication Data

Miller, Nathan R.
Teaching in circles : my journeys in teaching high school / Nathan R. Miller.
    p. cm.
ISBN 978-1-4277-9779-7
1. High school teaching--United States. I. Title.
LB1607.5.M55 2009
373.11020973--dc22

2008030637

10 9 8 7 6 5 4 3 2 1

ISBN-13: 978-1-4277-9779-7

Kaplan Publishing books are available at special quantity discounts to use for sales promotions, employee premiums, or educational purposes. Please email our Special Sales Department to order or for more information at kaplanpublishing@kaplan.com, or write to Kaplan Publishing, 1 Liberty Plaza, 24th Floor, New York, NY 10006.

To my students for inspiring me to write,
and my dear wife Kimberly for keeping me sane.

ACKNOWLEDGMENTS

Warm thanks to Larry Sutin and Mary Rockcastle for their early encouragement. Thank you to Neil Salkind and Michael Sprague for believing in me, and a special thank-you to my family and all teachers past—even the bad ones.

CONTENTS

I am still a learner, not a teacher, feeding somewhat omnivorously, browsing both stalk and leaves; but I shall perhaps be enabled to speak with more precision and authority by and by, — if philosophy and sentiment are not buried under a multitude of details.

~ *Henry David Thoreau*

NOTE

It is difficult to write in too much detail about individual students before violating their rights to privacy. Out of respect for that concern, all student names have been changed or left out completely. Identifying features may be altered slightly, but this has been done only in ways that do not change the accuracy of any events described. In rare cases, students who are mentioned briefly have been combined to avoid extra complication. Many names of adults have been changed, as well, out of respect for their privacy . . . and so I can still show my face at work.

CHAPTER I

Meet the Machine

J UST IN CASE PEOPLE FORGET what they are concerned about, every election cycle produces a flurry of polls reminding voters of their most pressing issues. Inevitably, regardless of leftist, centrist, or right-leaning tendencies, respondents list education near the top— usually right behind security and taxes. And why shouldn't they? The public education system in America is massive. People *should* be concerned about schools. After all, according to the National Center for Education Statistics, right now one in every six Americans is enrolled in kindergarten to grade 12 in our Nation's public schools. The Department of Education estimates that local, state, federal, and private spending on public schools nationwide added up to $909 billion in the 2004–2005 school year. Even if one takes the social implications out of the equation, schools are gargantuan by simple virtue of their proliferation and their share of the collective pot of tax-revenue funds. In plainer terms, schools are a big deal.

Add back in the social implications and the stakes are unparalleled. What can a society possibly value more than its children? What greater goal can a generation aspire than to make life as good as possible for the next generation? True, schools are but one force in a child's development, along with family, friends, and community. A person is not defined by—character is not determined by—the life one leads from kindergarten to diploma, but to suggest that schools do not carry incredible influence is to underestimate what happens there on a daily basis.

That's what I keep thinking about: what happens in schools on a daily basis. Politicians from both ends of the political spectrum use education as key components in their rhetoric and campaigns. Those millions of current students have millions of parents and guardians who wonder just how much school life has really changed since back in their day. Major laws are passed, mandated tests are conducted, and results are posted for scrutiny in newspapers and elsewhere. Television gives viewers such ridiculously inaccurate depictions of the school experience as Disney's *High School Musical*, *The OC*, *Boston Public*, and *Saved by the Bell*. All these people and ventures have a vested interest in schools, particularly high schools, yet few of them have a faint notion of true daily life. It is simpler and more complex than outsiders imagine it, and it is less sensational and even more melodramatic than depicted in the media. Perhaps outsiders with this vested interest will see fit to learn a little more about this curious thing called "high school" before becoming self-proclaimed experts.

As much as outsiders need a chance to look in, insiders need a chance to look around. Despite the highly social and interactive nature of education, the demands of all school-related jobs give their members a certain myopia—an inability to devote much of their precious time thinking about how they fit into the grand scheme of this huge system. For all the daily contact with others, it mysteriously feels like lonely work. Collegiality works wonders, and I have found virtual collegiality through sharing the following experiences with you. Everyone thinks they know what's going on with our kids—our schools—but the ones who shout the loudest often know the least. For those who proclaim to have the answers to those wanting an insider's view to those who simply need to commiserate, here is what I see from my little cog in the giant educational machine.

CHAPTER 2

Ultra-Negative Me

A SHOP TEACHER WITH 30 YEARS OF EXPERIENCE stops at my classroom door to chat for a moment before he reveals that he signed the paperwork to retire at the end of the year. The last thing he says is, "I'm telling you, though, I couldn't have made it this long if it was always like this. You have no idea how good it was." Two days later he leaves school at noon in an ambulance, having suffered a mild stroke. While he seems to be doing well now, nothing about a stroke of any kind seems mild to me.

I think teachers age at an accelerated rate. At 32 years old, I sound and feel like a crotchety old man on the front porch yelling at neighborhood kids to stay off my lawn. The top three prescription drugs purchased by the teachers in my district are a blood-pressure medication, an antacid, and an antidepressant. By that list, I've got one strike against me. I fear I'll need the other two drugs all too soon, and then I'll be out. My body will officially suffer as much as my psyche.

The shop teacher's words reverberate in my head all the time. He's been teaching for 30 years and may very well die before retirement.

Can I see myself teaching for 30 years? Forty? And how much should I believe him when he talks about how good it used to be? After all, memories can be wicked pranksters, selective in their accuracy and fickle about their clarity. This notion seems to be an underlying theme of political debates about education as well. Have the schools gone astray? Do we need to rope them in so we can return to the good old days?

I dismiss any banter about the good old days. I doubt they were so great as people claim simply because I don't trust memory. I personally can't even remember how many days last winter were really cold—were there more cold days than usual? How many times did I have to wear the down-filled parka? Just like trying to recall the daily temperature last winter, lamenting the loss of the golden age of education is use-less because it simply does not matter. It seems to me a more press-ing issue to look to where we are heading than to bicker over where we have been. Where we're heading scares me. The kids are broken, the schools are impotent, the families are clueless, and the politicians are misguided.

Of course times change. Of course our society is in a constant state of reinventing itself. Something happened, though. Something that seems to have set us all on a certain trajectory that may not be the one we would have chosen. We were wounded once and are in a perpetual state of building up scar tissue.

The scar tissue shows up in the form of emotional chaos and behavioral abnormalities. One could argue that the numbers are simply a result of greater awareness and more accurate diagnoses, but everything is on the rise: attention-deficit hyperactive disorders, emotional-behavioral disorders, oppositional-defiant disorders, obsessive-compulsive disorders, bipolar disorders, autism-spectrum syndromes, violent tendencies, drug abuse tendencies, attachment disorders, overt sexual behaviors, depression, and suicidal tendencies. Picture a spectrum with all of these kids in need of mental and/or emotional support at one end, and the so-called happy, well-adjusted kids at the other end. Regardless of the actual numbers of students, the end of the spectrum with all of these needs is heavier. It's denser. It rightfully requires more resources. These are my kids. I try to teach them about sentence structure, and it means nothing to them.

These are your kids too. These are not the kids that the privileged class can dismiss as unfortunate urban souls. For all the problems that accompany poverty and racism in urban settings, suburban schools aren't in much better shape. Maybe the test scores are higher. Maybe the graduation rate is higher. In fact, maybe the sports teams are better and the plays are better attended. But when it comes to what matters most, what's really hard to see and measure, all schools are pretty much equal: they are all full of broken kids.

Good kids, but damaged. For the last four consecutive years, I've had four consecutive 15-year-old girls hospitalized for attempted suicide. I've had my life threatened several times, once or twice when I truly became afraid. I've watched brilliant minds turn sluggish from pot. I've watched kids go through multiple hair, clothing, and piercing styles trying to find an identity. And every year I see a class leave and a new one arrive. The cattle corral shuffles them through just slowly enough that I can get a good look before they move on.

I probably ought to do something to help these broken kids. Instead, I sit and scratch my head like a confused chimpanzee. Sounds good in theory, but how?

It is my infuriating lot in life to embody lofty visions of grandeur pitted against a lazy disposition. I want to change the world and be an inspiration to my students, but that doesn't seem to be happening on its own. I also don't seem to be rushing out to make it happen. I could be better. That's not just a statement of modesty; I'm a firm believer in the infinite possibility for improvement, and yet I stay the same. Perhaps it's an incurable case of laziness. Maybe it's owed to arrogance. Maybe it's because I'm only a good teacher.

A quote that has stuck with me, despite my best efforts to tune out or disregard all motivational messages, is from Henry Ford: "The easier it is to be good, the harder it is to be great." I'm afraid he was right.

Throughout my life I see evidence supporting Ford's claim. Schoolwork came easily to me, so I didn't try that hard. Working in the theater, at first as an actor, felt effortless, so I gave it little effort. I have been blessed with intelligence and generous talents, but instead of achieving greatness I depend on these traits to help me get by with as little effort as possible.

I have no problem accepting my flaws. I dream big, I start projects I eventually abandon, my organizational skills consist of knowing which pile of papers contains the document I need, and I always take on more than I can handle. I could refute the laziness label if I really wanted to. I could play the overextended martyr. As I write this, I am teaching 150 students full time, trying to give them reasonably useful feedback on their formal writing skills and teaching them the lasting impact Homer's epic poetry had on Western storytelling. I am trying to attend meetings for my nearly 30 special-education students. I am designing a set for a major musical production and supervising a student crew that will construct it in the span of three weeks, using enough lumber to build a small house. I am co-supervising the design and layout of the school's annual literary arts journal. I am serving on a committee to revise the ninth- grade English curriculum for all four district high schools. I am trying (and failing) to spend as much quality time with my wife and two children as possible. I am selling my house so I can move closer to my job, eliminating the hour or more a day I spend in my car when I could be putting that time (and gas money) to better use.

True, I have the convenient excuse of having a lot on my plate. I could depend on that, but there's still the question of why I take on so much. The money? That helps, but there certainly are easier ways to earn money. Maybe not physically easier, but surely jobs that are easier in terms of mental and emotional exhaustion must be out there somewhere. I do these things because I love them all, yet I know I'm not doing anyone any favors. I take on as many jobs as I can, anyway. There is a chance that overextending myself, taking on too much, could actually be a form of laziness. That notion seems counterintuitive, I know, but hear me out. My red badge of overexertion gives me a certain leniency—permission to give subpar performances. Miller doesn't have those papers corrected yet? That's okay—he's been so busy with building the set. He doesn't have the set done yet? That's okay—he's been so busy with the literary journal.

Using all of these demands on my time as an excuse is pathetic, because I am not the only one stretched too thin. The causes of my predicament may be unique, but the state of being on the verge of a total collapse is a common one throughout education. We look at each other, shaking our heads, wondering how we're going to make it through the rest of the year, the coming years, the rest of our careers, and then we shrug, laugh, and say something like, "Only seven more Mondays till summer." Other teachers are taking graduate courses. Other teachers are coaching and advising activities. Others have families.

They have students with needs, monumental and urgent needs that could never be met by one individual teacher, and yet many of them try. Others have given up trying, content to believe that enough other teachers are taking a crack at each kid; hopefully one of them will make a difference. It sounds like a way of passing the buck, but really it's an essential coping mechanism. It's the only way to avoid feeling like a complete and utter failure for not turning a kid's life around during the 12 weeks of an academic trimester, the 50 minutes a day you had him or her along with 30 other kids in the room.

Simply put, I can't quite ever figure out just how I feel about teaching. For the nine years I have taught high school English, I have felt as though I have either one of the best or one of the worst possible jobs ever. I've felt like a professional with great integrity and a minion whose sole purpose is to be abused by others. Talking with others, those in teaching as well as in vastly different lines of work, it's apparent that waxing and waning passion about one's career is common. It's rare for someone to absolutely hate or love every aspect of his or her profession, yet something about my slippery relationship with my life as a teacher pesters me, pleads with me to be understood—or at least explored.

If the average person were to track his or her emotional perspective of any job, perhaps the baseline would be something like "content" and would have peaks and valleys ranging from "fulfilling" to "boring." Many teachers I know have a baseline of "exhausted" with peaks of "rewarding" and valleys of "depressing." I see myself as falling anywhere from God's gift to education to the biggest sham ever, with most of my teaching days spent somewhere in- between, around ambivalent or apathetic. In essence, the issues boil down to this one little question: Should I be teaching?

Other questions I face as a teacher are a little more nuanced and just as difficult to answer. These questions include: Why teach? What got me into this field? What's keeping me in the teaching profession? What's pushing me away? The beauty of these specific questions is that they allow for me to respond through example. You want to know something that's keeping me here, well, let me tell you about so-and-so. You want to know why I want to run out the door screaming and never come back? Well, let me tell you about this time when. . . . I'm looking for answers to questions I'm still trying to form.

I am highly suspicious of anyone who claims to have a clue of what's going on in America's schools today. The whole public education system is a country onto itself, with successes and failures so tightly intertwined that there simply isn't any one way to categorize anything about it. Complexity doesn't sell, though. People don't like intertwined. Buzzwords, catch phrases, and sound bites are much more palatable to a society that has other things to worry about. If a sure sign of wisdom is admitting how little one really knows, to me the wisest teachers are the ones willing to admit they don't have all the answers.

Is there a problem here? Are schools failing to serve our nation's kids? What about testing? And funding? And vouchers? And accountability? I have opinions on these questions and many more, but I should warn you that I have no answers. Absolutely none. And it drives me to the brink of a meltdown.

I love my job. Now and then.

I despise my job. A little too often.

Oftentimes, I'm just too drained to care.

There's a monster in my classroom, and I fear that it may be me. There's a monster in all our schools, and I fear it may eat us all alive. Like some Jekyll and Hyde creature, I possess equal power to help or hurt every student I encounter. Whenever I feel confident in my abilities, some kid with an acid tongue cuts me back down to size. It can be more than a little disheartening to give so deeply of oneself without any evidence to cease the nagging sense of futility. Zoom out from the close-up of my class, my school, my district, and state, region, and country. See how the giant system plays out the same confusing games on smaller scales in buildings everywhere. My experience, my quiet suburban school, is just like the kid in class who quietly does everything well. It's not the troublemaker or the overachiever. We do pretty well by most anyone's standards, but there's still something missing. When it's not a matter of privilege or poverty, when the school cannot be cast aside as a doomed, irreparable inner-city school, it just doesn't draw much attention to itself. But there are problems in idyllic suburbia too. They may not be as obvious or even as dire as our scapegoat counterparts downtown, but that's exactly why there's no high-level dialogue about it. Maybe a shooting occurs, and everyone talks about bullying for a while, but then it's back to the routine. The tiny catastrophes occurring daily chip away at the health of everyone inside: students, teachers, administrators, everyone.

There's a good chance you were a product of a public school, since over 90 percent of us were. Perhaps your kids are in school, or maybe you're a teacher yourself. Even if you've only ever set foot in the halls of private institutions, your life in our existence as we know it leaves you surrounded by us public school creatures. Education, schools, teaching . . . this all adds up to a matter of great significance, and yet we're all in a fog. We're all kidding ourselves into thinking there is an endless supply of problems and solutions to every aspect of education. Always tinkering, always calling for reform, always seeking some ambiguous higher standard. I find it demeaning to picture myself as an ass unsuccessfully pursuing a carrot that others—the ones who suspiciously claim to have answers—dangle before me.

Despite the burnout, the confusion, the fog, somewhere deep within me I know I can't let myself get so cynical as to abandon the will to at least explore what it's all about. Call it whatever buzz phrase you want (how about *reflective practice* or *self-efficacy* or some other hollow phrase that makes me giggle), but when I look back on my experience so far, and wonder how much longer I'll last, I believe I have something to offer. Despite all the reasons I want to run out the front door screaming deliriously, never to return, I don't.

I am nine years into a job I only expected to last one. Previously, my first full year as a teacher came to a close with a brutal lesson. Budget cuts: You're expendable. We'll need to keep the crazy woman who has her English classes beat sticks together as an hour-long lesson instead of you—best wishes and lots of luck. I was anxious to nab a new position anywhere, so I was relieved when my layoff was followed by an offer to teach at a moderate-sized high school at the opposite end of the Twin Cities metro area from my first school.

In many ways the new school turned out to be a mirror image of the old. It is an older building in a geographic area surrounded by new buildings. My school is reinventing itself constantly. It's skirting social disaster as the modest neighborhoods from the town's countryside days collide with the upscale developments catering to those seeking the new frontiers of the outer suburbs, creating an environment of old versus new and haves versus have-nots. Even though the school's identity as a mutating community was eerily reminiscent of the northern suburb of St. Francis and my initiation year into the teaching profession at St. Francis High School, I decided a paycheck is a paycheck.

When the call came, I decided I was willing to give the school a try until something better came along. Nine years later, I still wonder if something better will ever come along. Is this the best I can do for myself, or am I doomed to be a chronic malcontent—incapable of ever being satisfied?

Usually when people ask me why I became a teacher, my first response is that I couldn't resist the respect and adoration students shower on their teachers, and the pay was going to put me in a mansion by the time I was 30. This is not the answer I give in job interviews. I might flippantly spit that kind of comment out when my students ask, though. An outspoken young girl once recognized my sarcasm and evasiveness for what it was. She had the good sense to call me on my negativity and try to put an end to my whining.

"Why did you really go into it, then, if all you ever do is complain? Why don't you do something else if you hate it so much?"

Slightly ashamed, I began the real explanation. I had some wonderful teachers in my own school experience who made a difference, and I wanted to emulate them.

I didn't tell her everything, like how my sixth-grade teacher was one of those key figures. He taught the class with humor, he rarely seemed to have bad days, and he took a special interest in providing extra challenges for a friend of mine and me. While the rest of the class was studying their states and capitals, the two of us sat with him at a table in the corner of the room discussing satire in George Orwell's *Animal Farm*.

One spring day, while lining up at the door (remember getting into lines?), I decided to share with him one of my sibling's favorite little gags. It would start off by shaking a person's hand and saying,

"Hi. I work at the hardware store. We sell hammers [the handshake simulating hammering], saws [with the handshake motion turning to a back-and-forth sawing motion] . . . and paintbrushes." At that point I was to let go of the person's hand and lightly slap the victim back and forth across the face. My brother had done it to me dozens of times. My teacher was laughing and smiling along as I went. I got to the paintbrush part and made sure I was extra gentle as my fingers flapped on both sides of his chin. Apparently being gentle didn't matter. It's amazing how quickly a person, even only 11 years old, can realize he's made a terrible mistake.

I sat alone with him in the room while the rest of the class went to recess. He chastised me for striking a teacher, and I flushed with embarrassment even though he was careful to do it gently and away from the rest of the class. I still turn red and get a lump in my throat when I remember that day. What does it mean when those who inspired me leave me with memories evoking shame?

I still frequently think of that girl who, five years ago, asked me why I still teach when all I ever do is complain about it. Her question bumps into me when I least expect it, walking through a crowded hallway, sitting for an hour guarding an entrance like a bouncer, cleaning up mountains of bottles, wrappers, papers, and crap left on the floors of the vast compound comprising our high school. I'm haunted by old insecurities about my effectiveness. I'm angered by the political rhetoric, the student apathy, and the trivial silliness of meetings and forms and procedures that I suppose must accompany any line of work and contribute nothing to the job at hand.

I can vividly see my supervisor sitting across a circle from me ten years ago when, during a seminar with other student teachers, the man with a gentle face and muddy voice pointed out to us that more teachers leave the profession within their first three years on the job than any other profession. I recall the nervous chuckles and tentative smiles we all gave him, not quite sure if he was warning us or giving us a challenge to rise above. Beneath the calmly uncertain exterior, though, a much more hysterical reaction was beginning: What the fuck do I do now?

Painted cinder blocks. That's my domain, my classroom. The generic blocks with the listless paint could be from any school, anywhere. I do have one visual source of beauty, though: a large window next to my desk looking out into an enclosed courtyard in the center of the building. I oftentimes think I should hang a bird feeder in the tree right outside my window—a stout flowering tree of some sort—but for some reason I never seem to do it. It's typical of me and just as well, because if I actually did put a bird feeder out there I would have to deal with the guilt of not ever filling it. In fact, I rarely get a chance to look out the window at all, because my blinds are usually down. Apparently at some point in the high school's hundred-plus-year history, orange was a popular motif for the building. The only remnants now are the handful of rooms with muted rusty orange blinds instead of the less offensive navy blue ones everywhere else. I have the orange blinds and choose to leave them down because it's an absolute battle to raise and lower them. The blinds are metal and full of bends and dings. A few of them stick together because I once left a can of soda against the window to cool over a winter weekend and returned Monday morning to find it had exploded. The glare from the uncovered window makes it nearly impossible to clearly see the television mounted in the opposite corner of the room. It occurs to me that I don't use the television that much, but when the blinds have been left down for awhile it's hard to remember that there's reason to open them.

Every summer the heating and cooling unit fills with insects and pumps in a mass of stale, humid air. The bugs are my welcoming committee when I return in August for the occasional meeting before fall workshop kicks off. The insects, giant flying ants it seems, run rampant for a couple of weeks and then die off. One fall I swatted one against the wooden valance over the window with a grammar workbook. The flattened bug stuck to the valance, where it remained for the next two years.

Keys carry an incredible sense of power. I worked as a security officer on campus when I was in college, and I think the ability to come and go from any room I wanted was what drew me to that otherwise miserable job. Given all the work I do with theater, how many given doors I might have to open just to accomplish a simple task, I have a master key to the school. Now, that's not nearly as special as it sounds, because virtually every head of any activity or sport has one, but I love my key regardless. I sometimes go exploring with my key to see what I can find. The building has a labyrinth of underground mechanical rooms full of intimidating machinery, pumps, and circuit breakers. One room resembles the lab of a mad scientist, complete with giant switches that Igor could be commanded to throw. Yes, I've tried it. I threw those switches with relish, feeling powerful from controlling so much power. Yes, I liked it. I remember vividly in my college security days walking from building to building in the dead of a winter night through underground tunnels used to run steam pipes to the heating systems of each building ("Watch your heads," the engineers would laugh, "a steam leak down here can have enough pressure to slice your head clean off!"), and the boyish feeling of adventure I felt then returns when I explore the bowels of my current school.

Slowly but surely every door in the building is being converted to keyless ID tag entry. My access will be computer programmed and monitored to limit me to the doors I reasonably need to open, and my exploring days will most likely come to a halt. I don't know how much longer I'll play this game.

I would have given up on the job long ago if it weren't for the theater program. I was drawn in as a child, producing, directing, and starring in sloppy performances with a cast of classmates loaned to me by my elementary school teachers who sent me out into the hall to rehearse while others had story time.

In junior high, I watched classmate after classmate stumble over reading *Tales of a Fourth Grade Nothing* during an audition. Students hate reading out loud in front of their peers, and the insecurity they often feel tends to be the source of their problems. My ability to fluently make heads or tails of cold readings without sounding like a blundering idiot brought me to the forefront of productions unusually elaborate for junior high schools. I also benefited from being substantially taller than many of my peers, so I was more likely to play a leading man, an adult, than the shrimpy-boy alternatives. By high school I had the advantage of my previous years of experience, and I continued to excel as a leading actor. In college, though, a drastic change that had been lurking beneath the surface broke through. I became painfully introverted—reluctant to get to know new people and lacking confidence in my performing. I lost the advantages I had during the previous years and auditioned for shows I didn't get in. My overinflated ego took an excessive pendulum swing in the opposite direction, as depression and anxiety attacks that had begun in high school threatened to take a destructive grip.

All was not lost, though. My fall from a life of performing opened the doors to other aspects of theater. I knew going into college that I was not up for the ruthless life of a starving professional actor, yet I wanted to keep my connection to the art. I had planned all along to go into education as a way to live a life of plays while having a reliable source of food for the table. In order to teach theater, I was going to need to know more than acting. It turns out that writing is an outstanding outlet for a neurotic introvert. Turns out that directing is a fine job for someone who has always loved manipulating situations. And tech is a beautiful match for masochists who enjoy lurking in dark corners.

Now, whether I am the director shaping an entire production or the tech director designing and building a set, every show provides deep personal satisfaction while aging me prematurely at the same time.

Our theater, which until last year was the youngest part of our piecemeal building, is my home away from home. The wood stage floor, once a rich dark walnut, is excessively worn, scuffed, scratched, and splattered despite its relatively young age—a sure sign of the weight of our work. The 650 maroon seats are in continental seating rows, meaning there are only aisles at the outside ends. The intent is to make the audience feel like they're part of a collective, that they're participating in the group activity that is viewing a live performance. Much like a laugh track on a sitcom trying to subconsciously erase one's loneliness, the intent of continental seating is to avoid creating divides that make an audience member feel—even at the subconscious level—a sense of isolation. That's the intent, anyway. The actual result is that every row has to have a lot of leg room for emergency evacuation purposes. With my long legs I love this feature, but others despise it because the effect on the aisles on either side of the house is that steps are completely irregular. There are little steps going down from one row to the next, and big steps that serve as a mini-landing at each row. Many patrons have stumbled their way down the steps, including one elderly woman who actually tumbled and rolled down a few steps. I thought that disaster might lead to the installation of adequate aisle lighting. As it is, little dim lights show the set of steps at every other row. It can sometimes be just as enjoyable to watch latecomers with eyes unadjusted to the darkness fumble along the aisle, clutching the handrail for dear life, than to watch the play itself.

Sometimes, if I'm directing, I sit in the middle of the house to run a rehearsal. I prefer seat M19. I chose it by accident one day, as I walked up the irregular steps over halfway back and over to the center. The M was fitting for Miller, and 19 coincided nicely with the center of the house and a childhood baseball hero. Of course, I don't ever tell people that. I just drift back to get some perspective on the stage, much more a creature of habit than I'll ever readily admit. Sometimes, if I'm playing the technical director role, I sit in the control booth and help kids program lighting instruments and run the sound equipment. Other times I'm in the scene shop praying for another day of set construction without any students losing appendages. Sometimes I'm under the house in a basement—level green room—a combination of dressing rooms, makeup counters, lounge area, and rehearsal space. Anyone can feel theatrical stepping into that room with incredibly reverberant acoustics off the concrete floor and brick walls. Even the wimpiest voice sounds rich and commanding. And who can resist full-wall mirrors with rows of bare bulb lighting? Many incredible kids have transformed themselves in this very room before presenting their new, fictitious identities to a sympathetic audience of parents, classmates, and teachers.

Sometimes I work in the catwalks, dozens of feet over the house of the theater. Every step on the plywood walkway is unique. Sometimes the wood is coming loose from the welded frame below it, making a loud slap with each step. Other times scraps of old carpet have been laid down to try and muffle the clamor of footsteps. The whole system is enclosed with wire fencing in an effort to instill a sense of security, and I believe it works as I am normally terrified of heights but find myself quite comfortable in the catwalks. Curved maroon facades provide a decorative underbelly to the catwalk system high over the audience's heads. As long as I've worked in the building, a handful of monstrous spitballs have been plastered on these ceiling panels. I keep expecting to glance up one day and noticed they've disappeared—fallen off by mere chance—or (yes, just maybe, yes) actually cleaned off by someone.

Not yet.

CHAPTER 3

Ultra-Positive Me (Well, Mostly Positive Me)

E VEN AS I FIND MYSELF BITTERLY TRANSFORMING from idealistic newcomer to burned-out veteran, I cannot entirely let go of the positive. I would even go so far as to say that somewhere, deep in my core, a glimmer of that idealist still hides. Most people who know me would find such a claim laughable, but if I search honestly, it's clear I still believe in these basic tenets:

- Everyone—students and teachers—has an infinite capacity to grow, develop, learn, and improve.
- Most students want to succeed and, even though I complain about their resistance to anything requiring effort, most enjoy learning.
- A lot of teachers are doing some pretty amazing work with their classes.

Now, while you try to reconcile what I've just stated here with the unabashed negativity of the previous chapter, let me clarify just a little bit. I believe everyone has an infinite capacity to grow and learn, but most settle far short of their potential. Most students want to succeed and enjoy learning, but schools are losing the battle to many of the distractions vying for students' time, energy, and interests. A lot of teachers are doing some pretty amazing work, but much of it goes unappreciated. Apparently I have a hard time remaining positive for too long.

CHAPTER 4

Crashing Techies

I N MY THEATER, I am king among a mob of the socially peculiar. My mob is fiercely loyal, relentless in their work ethic, and awkward beyond belief. In return, I am fiercely loyal to them. I do my best to keep up with their energy, and I show them that an awkward person can lead a normal life. These are the faithful who follow me into the trenches of building a show. The techies.

These strange creatures feed on the darkness of backstage, the ingratitude of actors who receive all the accolades, the scars that come with injuries received in the line of techie duties. The kids talk about harrowing experiences with pride while I continue to cringe. Crash, a feisty ninth-grade girl helping to build the set for *Lès Misérables*, got her nickname from an accident that still makes me shudder. I was out on the stage with several students providing guidance on various projects. I walked back into the shop and entered the adjacent office. Minutes later, someone ran in telling me Crash had fallen. The few minutes I was in another room were just enough time for some particularly immature boys to start causing trouble with her. It turned into a childish sort of flirting, almost, with the three of them all throwing things and chasing each other around the stage. As Crash ran from the boys, she managed to run over a 24-inch square opening in the floor. We had painstakingly re-created a panel of hardwood flooring to match the rest of the stage right over the orchestra pit. This panel, unlike the normal one, had the square cut out for a trapdoor. Problem was, we were at the point where we had the trap but not the trapdoor.

The area should have been marked off. There should have been cordons. A large piece of plywood would have been a suitable cover. I didn't have any of those things in place, though, because we were working on hinging the door for the opening. We were working on that part of the stage at that very moment. Well, not at that exact moment. At that exact moment, I was in the next room and Crash was falling eight feet to the concrete floor below. The size of the opening being what it was, there was the very real possibility she hit her face or head on the way down.

I peered down from above and saw her lying facedown against the unforgiving gray floor. Her arms were out to the sides like a cliché chalk outline from the old cop shows. She was moaning but not moving. I sent one student to track down the director holding rehearsal in another part of the school. I sent another student to see if the athletic trainer was around, as her office was near the theater facilities. She came in and quickly assessed the situation, determining that Crash definitely had a concussion, needed to have her arms checked, and ought to be carried out on a board with her neck immobilized when paramedics came.

I was grateful when a police officer who had arrived on the scene early offered to call Crash's parents. I don't know what I would have said. I don't ever want to know what I would actually say in that situation. The trainer and the police officer glanced at me every so often as they talked to each other and to Crash. Every time they looked my way, I was sure I was being judged. Looks can shame, and feelings of guilt can make those dirty looks even more potent. I felt like everyone was looking at me: worried students, the trainer who handled the situation I couldn't control, the police officer whose very presence made me feel like I had done something wrong, and the paramedics who barely had time to notice me as they hauled Crash out on a board with her neck in a collar.

I stopped by the hospital on my way home that night, hoping for some good news. Her skull was okay. It seemed the ponytail she was wearing actually cushioned the blow to the back of her head on her way through the opening. A ponytail that day saved her from untold damage. The remaining concern, though, was her jaw. It was exceptionally sore where her face hit the concrete, so there was still some concern that it may have been broken. As soon as I saw her in the hospital bed, unable to open her mouth while she rested between CAT scans, I decided on the spot that I would eat through a straw as long as she had to. To this day I'm not sure if it was some form of penance to cope with the guilt I felt, or if I actually felt a need to display a compassionate act of empathy. I also don't know if I would have actually followed through with my silent vow, since I have already mentioned I am notorious for not finishing what I start, because I never had to do it. Her jaw wasn't broken.

The kids I work with, whether as the fiercely loyal masochist misfits or the semblances of my former glory as a performer, give of themselves to an extent that redeems my hope for the next generation. The actors fill me with nostalgia and admiration for how much better they are than I ever was, even though I didn't know it at the time. The techies are a marvel. Their sacrifices are even greater than the actors'.

They give of their time, their sleep, and their well-being without anything close to the recognition the performers get. At 1:00 AM I sit shaking my head in amazement that there are six kids with me, just as happy to be painting a set as doing anything else their peers might be up to on a Friday night.

Now and then an actor stops me in my tracks. Not just because of his or her abilities, but because he embodies everything I was and wished I could have been. Then, of course, he moves on and I stay. As inspiring as these kids are, it can be utterly depressing to see them go.

For Example:

I'm sitting in an old armchair. It's no wonder someone donated it—it's not fit for any home. The chartreuse upholstery is ripped on the arms and stained brown across the back. As I sit, though, it's as good as a throne. I pull the chair forward a few feet, dragging the peg legs across the concrete floor, generating a hollow scraping sound that reverberates off the cinder block walls, sending chills from the back of my neck to my fingertips. I settle into my dusty throne, cross my legs, and hold my pen to my torn sheet of yellow legal paper. Matthew is standing directly in front of me—a bundle of energy slowed down only by having gotten up earlier than college life has him accustomed to. Nobody else is here. Of course it feels like many others are here, because our reflections in the full-wall mirrors shine back on one another infinitely with endless duplications of ourselves that we barely even notice anymore. We laugh and joke and talk like old times and then get serious. He walks to the door and walks back to the space before me with a gentle smile, scanning an imagined audience around the room. He introduces himself, transforms his voice and stature before my very eyes, and switches from mild student to jesting fool in the moment of a deep inhale. Watching him, I remember how much I like the color of his hair—slippery shades of brown that sometimes looks auburn, copper, or simply brown depending on the angle and the light. I am reminded of where he came from—a transfer student three years ago tentatively feeling out a new school full of strangers. I think of how he convinced an entire school that boys weren't automatically gay because they studied dance. I look back and see him as a sailor and a cowboy and a friar and a stonecutter and a fugitive and a writer. I look ahead and see him going places with his gift that I could only have dreamed about at his age. Here he stands before me with low-hanging pants exaggerating his already long torso. His arms sway freely without flailing. His mouth contorts, and spit pools up inside his lip. He's moved on but come back for a moment, come back for some coaching, but I suspect it's just as much for my benefit as it is for his. At least, that's how it feels. I sit in my tattered chair, basking in the glow of his abilities for which I cannot take credit, here in the green room that is anything but green, and there's nobody here but us, sitting and talking. With every question he asks, every thought of insecurity he expresses, every nervous gesture he makes, I smile to myself, thinking *if only you knew how little you have to worry about.*

At that very moment, I know this isn't just my job; it's my vocation—my calling. Then he leaves for New York and I go back to my classroom.

CHAPTER 5

Swearing boy

I FIRST BEGIN TO FEEL like a crotchety old man when I catch myself wanting to use the word *hoodlum*. I mentally berate myself for even thinking to myself in such a term, yet the huddle of grunting, chuckling, profanity-spewing teenage boys blocking my way through a terrible bottleneck in the high school corridors evokes that very word. Punk isn't clear enough, *delinquent too* technical. *Little bastard* might suffice, but at that moment *hoodlum* keeps running through my head. Day after day, they stand in their little gang huddle, occasionally offering up comments loud enough for everyone in the hall to hear, sometimes just being a nuisance through their simple physical presence. I hate them.

Am I a prude? Certainly not. I can fucking swear as much as the next hoodlum. Damn, there's that word again. There is simply something about hearing that kind of language from kids—hearing it from kids all day long—and seeing no discretion or regret on their part when I am around. I would have cowered in humiliation if a teacher heard me say anything close to what kids casually (and effortlessly) spout off in my presence daily. Perhaps in and of itself, kids swearing is innocuous, but in the grand scheme of the modern high school it is one more sign of the decaying respect for teachers. I *know* they will swear, just as I know *I* will swear. Damn it, though, I want them to restrain themselves when I am around.

Someone, one of the hoodlums, I don't know which, lets a "fuck" fly loud enough for me to catch as I head past the huddle. *I am in a good mood*, I remind myself. *I don't need to make a big deal out of this*, I say to myself. *Don't pick a fight, but don't let it go unacknowledged, either.*

I stop. I smile. I turn to the hoodlums in their little hooligan huddle. They stop their talking; some turn to me.

This should just take a second, I think.

"You know," I say as positively as I can, "just once I would like to have a day when I can walk up and down these halls and not hear any swearing. Do you think you could help me out with that?" I scan the faces looking dumbly back at me. A couple of the smug sons of bitches laugh. I know one of them from a class the year before. He won't make eye contact. *God, they piss me off. Best to leave it at that and get back to the day's tasks at hand. I made my point; I let them know I could hear them.*

"Maybe another day," one of the little bastards spits out through laughs over his shoulder, not even able to turn fully to look me in the eye. A well of heat and fury rises from my gut and finds a home in my clenched jaw, refusing to allow his challenge to go unmet. I grab the little weasel by the shoulder strap of his backpack and spin him around to face me.

"You seem to have mistaken my rhetorical question for an opportunity to offer your own response. I don't want to hear any response from you."

The ratface isn't impressed by my show. Instead, he stands in total disbelief that I made him turn around by touching his precious backpack. "What the hell? Don't touch me, man," is his eloquent response. I immediately realize I am treading dangerous ground. *I didn't touch him; I touched his bag.* It was an aggressive move, though, and all his hoodlum friends saw it. *Don't let this escalate.*

"Watch it."

"Don't touch me again or I'll beat the crap out of you!" he threatens.

Don't play into his escalation. "You are making this worse than it needs to be. All you have to do is nod or say okay, and I'll just keep on walking. Why are you causing trouble?"

"You're the one causing trouble. You can't grab me like that. Touch me again and I'll kick your ass."

This isn't what I had in mind.

I wanted to have a clear conscience, knowing I had done my part to not turn a blind eye to the behavior all the teachers complain about, but this has gotten messy. I find myself wishing I had walked on by like any other day. Why did I suddenly decide I needed to say something to them? Too late at this point—I have to hold my ground.

"All right. You had your chance to cooperate. Let's go to the office."

"Yeah, I'll go to the office. I want to tell them all what you did to me!" My cheeks burn. His statement, in turn, is followed by a chorus of support from the huddle of hooligans, all speaking out for their severely wronged friend. Angered and ridiculed, I know I am taking some definite chances as a nontenured teacher. Somehow I don't seem to care. Instantaneous scenarios involving lawyers and investigations, allegations of excessive roughness with students play out in my head. I have no job security then; I could be gone long before it comes to a formal lawsuit. And yet, as I walk with him, I am far more concerned about finishing what I started. If I have to put up with kids like this, maybe I wouldn't mind getting fired.

At least he is going to the office willingly, even if for different reasons than mine. I drop the kid off with the assistant principal in the hallway, give a quick explanation of what happened, and move on. I spent more time on this than I ever wanted to, and I am now late to my next class. I figure the kid would complain for a while, the AP won't have any of it, and then he'd end up with a detention or something. Detention itself is somewhat of a joke, because only the halfway decent kids bother to go and meet their obligation. The ones who deserve it the most skip without repercussion. *At least I didn't let him get away with it.*

I am sick with anxiety for a full hour after my unfortunate encounter with the hallway riffraff. I went too far. What if the AP believes him? I should have reported less about the swearing and more about the threats he made after that. It would make my little move with the shoulder strap pretty insignificant if he actually threatened me with intentional physical harm. *I am in trouble—no—why should I be in trouble when he's the one screwing up?*

Midday and I still haven't entirely forgotten the exchange, but I am no longer completely preoccupied with it. I let my class out for lunch, head down to the staff lounge, and commiserate with colleagues on the decline in discipline among students. The teachers sound old and tired; I am right there with them, though I do make a conscious effort to avoid the word *hooligan*. Heading back to my room, I look down the hall and see my class scattered about waiting for the door to be dutifully unlocked. Other students mix and mingle within my class, and a pair of strange boys emerge from their midst, heading my way as I head toward them. As we pass each other, they intentionally increase the volume of their conversation to make sure I plainly hear every *fuck*, *damn*, and *shit*. Somehow, with my mind focused on resuming class, I simply shake my head at their display and don't make the connection to this morning.

Surrounded by my own students as I unlock the door, one boy asks what the problem was with the two who just walked by. He tells me that they stopped outside my door and asked him and a couple other kids in class if I was their teacher. Of course, they didn't know me well enough to ask by name, so they described me as best they could: something along the lines of "the tall, wavy-haired guy with the goatee." When my students said I was their teacher, they responded with, "Yeah, we're going to kill him."

This is the second time I find myself worrying about a student wanting to kill me.

The first incident was within months of beginning my first full-time job. It was a small high school on the farthest reaches of suburban Minneapolis, almost to the point of being a rural setting. A young boy with a monstrous grudge against the world was helping me with tech work for a production of *Dracula*. At the Friday night performance he spent the entire evening making rude, insulting, and sexually harassing comments over the backstage intercom system, so I asked him not to return the next day.

Saturday morning I got a call from the director. She had received word that the boy in question was missing. The boy's mother called to warn us that she had no idea where he had gone, and that he apparently had taken his shotgun with him. The same shotgun, it turns out, that he had repeatedly threatened his stepfather with in the past. No one knew where he was, he had a gun, he was full of as much rage as any teenager I've encountered, and I was the last one to truly piss him off. Our lackluster production had been somewhat painful to sit through, anyway, but that night's performance was sheer agony. I didn't expect anything to happen, really, but what one expects and what one fears aren't always the same. A local police officer swept the building before we began for the evening, and the show concluded a few hours later without incident.

The boy turned up at school Monday morning as if nothing out of the ordinary had occurred, but I was left with the horrifying prospect of being afraid of the kids I was supposed to have authority over.

I attempt to think rationally and tell myself that these new hoodlums are just talking big, but the times don't allow for assumptions. It doesn't matter how rare school violence actually is; news footage of terrified students fleeing a building has been permanently ingrained in my imagination. I ask more and more of the class about what they heard the two say before I returned; I try to get the exact wording. Sweat forms on my forehead. My palms turn cold and clammy. Do I need to watch over my shoulder as I go out to my car after school? Even if they don't hurt me, will somebody be watching to find out which car in that vast parking lot is mine for future reference? How serious and dangerous are these . . . hooligans? No, *hooligan* is a funny word. I am not amused right now. How dangerous are these degenerates? Degenerates . . . it's not an amusing word, but it too makes me sound like an old man.

My day should be about reading and writing. Tell me about a good story you read. Write about a vacation for me. My days should be harmless, harmless. I remember my silent prediction, the one I don't share with anyone, regarding my 15 minutes of fame. I am certain, as I look from my desk in the back corner of the room to the chalkboard, and then through it into the future, that I can see myself being killed by a student. I'm not sure if he will be a student I have in class at the time (I do know it will be a boy—they always are), or if it will be a former student, or even some kid I don't even know. I don't know if he'll be out to get me, or if I'll be one casualty in the midst of a random massacre, but my gut is convinced I'll die in this building. It's irrational paranoia, sure, but it's my paranoia all the same. It's still what I live with. Perhaps it will be a boy I just met this morning in the hall.

A stroke of luck—by that afternoon, as I retell the whole day's events to a friend who teaches with me in the afternoon, he realizes who I am talking about and tells me the name of one of the two who made the threat. The name! As a teacher, nothing bolsters authority more than taking away the student's anonymity. Countless times I have seen something in passing—a kid kicking a bottle down the hall—and wished I could quickly intervene without taking too much time. If I simply say, "Could you pick that up, please?" I might be met with cooperation, but more often than not I am met with a scoff and a rapid departure. Kids know teachers are too tired, too downtrodden, to pursue them for trivial problems, and they know they can slip into obscurity around any corner. As many students as I will encounter during a year, there is no way to know all 2,000 of them. But now, now I know his name. Now he can't get away with it. I go down to the AP's office. I give him more details about the threat to kick my ass made by the first student this morning, which I am bringing up now in light of additional threats made by his friends this afternoon. He has a grave look. The issue has become substantially more serious. For a moment I wonder if he is angry with me for not telling him all the details until now, but if he is, he doesn't show it. He thanks me and assures me he'll look into it. By the end of the day, I am told all three boys involved will be suspended.

Through fate or coincidence, parent-teacher conferences are that night. Conferences are not as bad as most of my colleagues would have you believe. The time is not that big of a strain, and parents get a convenient opportunity to see all of their child's teachers in an evening. I relish the chance to meet and thank parents of the rare gems: the cooperative, motivated kids. I choose my words very carefully when a child is dropping the ball in class; you never know how the parents will reprimand him or her.

Swearingboy's parents have come in, and they would like to meet with the AP and me to get the whole story surrounding the suspension. This is a conversation I would rather not have. He's gone home and told them his side, I think. They'll be angry from his one-sided influence. They'll bring up the shoulder strap. I know it. I leave my table at conferences and walk down to the main office meeting room. I wait outside. I hear noisy exchanges but can't make out the words. The AP steps out and asks me to come in. I am introduced to the parents, and I shake their hands as I try to read their faces. They look so . . . normal, I think to myself. I expect to see some slobs waiting for me at the table. That would make so much more sense to me. Stupid, ugly parents would provide an explanation for the way Swearingboy behaved. These parents could just as easily have been my parents. The AP then instructs me simply to tell them what happened in my own words. I recap the whole encounter. I am honest and straightforward. I don't leave anything out. I beat the kid to the punch, just in case he's even thinking about bringing it up. . . .

". . . I know he wasn't happy with me when I gave him a tug on the backpack to turn him around and look at me, so I don't know if he's complained to you about that or not. I was simply trying to talk to him about his behavior. It's unfortunate it came to this."

I stop and breathe. My temples are throbbing. I glance back and forth from Mom, to Dad, to Swearingboy, and back again. I make fleeting eye contact with the boy. He shifts his glare away from me as soon as he sees a tiny, smug grin cross my lips. He may be tougher, my flicker of a smile tells him, but I have the System on my side. I do. Mom and Dad are appalled and apologize to me profusely. They tell me repeatedly how he wasn't raised that way, and how they are mystified about where this sort of behavior comes from. The AP thanks me for my time and excuses me to return to conferences. I leave the room feeling a stack of bricks has been lifted from my chest.

Swearingboy 2 has come up to the school, also during conferences, upon getting the phone message from the AP that he also has been suspended. Once again I am called from my table between meetings with parents to go and meet with the AP, this vulgar boy, and the boy's special-education case manager. I expect the same defiant glare that Swearingboy 1 gave me, but he is a little different. This is the one who told my class he would kill me, and now he sits before me with a red face and cap pulled down to hide as he hangs his head. He speaks quietly and won't make eye contact. He denies saying those things; it was all the other kid. The buck now stops with Swearingboy 3, aka Threatboy 2.

Apparently I have been called in to make sure I cannot directly contradict his statement, which I can't. I only know the little bit my students told me. I don't know which one said which things. I have also been called in so he can apologize to me, which he does sheepishly. This big kid who could easily kick my ass if he wanted to sits with his head lowered. He pulls his hat down so far I don't see his eyes during the entire apology. He still gets suspended for swearing at me, regardless of whether or not he made the threat.

I return to my table again, waiting for the last hour of conferences to dwindle to a close. I think about the two side meetings I have had that evening and wonder which parents I'll see before heading home. The insanity of the day—this long, taxing day—ends as unassumingly as it began. I exchange pleasantries with a handful of parents and leave for the night thinking that, for all the drama of the day, the job has a way of correcting its course when it starts to drift off the charts.

Three months later. It's nearly the end of second hour, and I've just spent 50 minutes watching an entrance to make sure no one comes or goes. I would really like to be most of the way back to my room before classes get out, so I leave my post a couple minutes earlier than I should. I take too long packing up my papers, though, and my timing is off. Now I am left to brave the gauntlet of a packed hallway. Suddenly I am not so different from a little ninth grader.

The bottleneck isn't too bad. I quicken my pace, hurry past the huddle, and keep my gaze fixed straight ahead. For their part, the hoodlums don't talk loudly enough for me to hear them. I'm grateful I have slipped by without incident, even though I can imagine what they're saying under their collective breath. I whisper to myself, "I am pathetic," in response to the fleeting thought that tomorrow I will take a different, roundabout route back to my room and avoid this hall. Near my classroom door, I look back over my shoulder to see if any of them has followed me. Back at the huddle, two of them quickly look down to the floor after a millisecond of eye contact. I unlock the door through heart palpitations and retreat to my room.

CHAPTER 6

Open Letter Number 1

D EAR GOVERNOR (AND OTHER LIKE-MINDED POLITICOS),

You, like many others throughout the country with a vested interest in public policy, hold a keen interest in "reforming" many facets of public education. After all, education and health care are the black holes of public expenditure. Anemic efforts to provide adequate funding in the past have given recent, current, and future politicians the unenviable task of trying to play catch-up. I'd consider you a victim of this predicament if you hadn't played such a key role in creating the problem during your years in the legislature. Each and every year that funding doesn't keep pace with the demands of running schools makes it that much harder to bite the bullet in the future. When you adopt a philosophy of no-taxes-for-anything-under-any-circumstances-come-hell-or-high-water, it makes matters even more complicated. Other methods to cut costs must be found.

One surefire way to fail miserably at saving money when it comes to education is to write a set of "clear" standards for all students at all grade levels in every subject area. That way, any teacher anywhere in the state will know exactly what she or he should be doing with his or her classes. To make failure even more likely, the standards will be a convoluted document that professes to avoid a state-mandated curriculum while telling every school in the state exactly what it must do. Then, just when every school district in the state has spent combined millions on aligning itself with the state's mandated standards (not to be confused with mandated curriculum), let's drop 'em like a bad habit. After all, we've got No Child Left Behind to think about.

President George W. Bush promoted his Federal Education Act—more commonly known as No Child Left Behind—as the solution to "soft" educational racism along with other unnamed teacher acts he presented as practically criminal. The law, also known as No Child Left Untested among teachers, is a hefty volume of legislation as entertaining and widely read as the unabridged USA PATRIOT Act. In fact, the entire text of the Federal Education Act is difficult to track down. Lots of snippet summaries can be found on various government websites, but no one seems to want a common person—a teacher, for example—to be able to get his or her hands on the whole darn document without a lot of effort. One thing's for certain, though: The private companies who make millions on contracts with districts and states to develop and score standardized tests are huge proponents of the law. And why shouldn't they be? They get a king's ransom to print booklets, run answer sheets through a machine, and send meaningless numbers to newspapers for praise or scorn (usually scorn) from a public who likes its analyses reduced to a number, letter, thumbs up or down, or certain number of stars/smiley faces/shaded dots. Thank goodness nobody actually tracks an individual student's scores throughout his or her education to ensure progress. That might get expensive. And make too much sense. And be too useful. Instead, entire grade levels of students will be tested and have the scores compared to an entirely different group of students: those who were in their grade the previous year. Any parent of multiple children should know that all kids are exactly the same, so it follows infallible logic to assume that if one child earns one score on a certain test, the next year another child should automatically do as well as (if not better than) his or her predecessor.

Of course, no good conversation on the merits of standardized tests is complete without extolling the virtues of alternative teacher pay and damning union-negotiated salary schedules. You, Governor, are conceptually quite fond of the notion of merit-based pay for teachers. Merit pay sounds good, right? After all, virtually every line of work offers some sort of financial reward to employees for a job well done. Even the words themselves are pleasant. *Merit.* Merit is good. And *pay.* I definitely like pay. Especially when it took me three years as a teacher to start earning a salary larger than the sum of my student loans upon graduating from college.

Ooh! And what better way to control those extravagant contract settlements that have ballooned beyond all control! Your acidic opinion seems to be that the automatic raises on the pay scale known as *steps* for years of experience and *lanes* for advanced education are nothing more than welfare for substandard teachers. Well, the single greatest factor that shapes a teacher's effectiveness, in my estimation, is that person's natural temperament and personality. Okay, so temperament and personality are actually two factors, not one, but what can you do? After a teacher's personality and temperament, however, the next most valuable trait is experience. Every minute of a teacher's career involves learning from students far more than teaching them. If that teacher is willing to think about what he or she learns every minute of every day of every year, then the potential exists for anyone who survives long enough to become a stellar teacher. My dear governor,

I can see why paying a teacher more for gaining more experience is purely wasteful.

The real problem with merit-based pay is that, as with most big-concept reform ideas, the devil is in the details. For example, merit-based pay is oftentimes pitched as a cost-saving measure. The unspoken message behind this claim is the implication that not very many teachers would be deserving of raises if they had to somehow "earn" them through merit. Governor, what if you and your ilk discovered a scenario you never imagined? What if you push a merit-based pay plan through, only to discover that thousands of teachers around the state deserve more than they currently get? You could wind up as a Prometheus figure, thinking you are doing good by bringing fire to the mortals, only to end up getting punished by the antitax deities you worship for opening the vaults to everyone who deserves raises, not just that lazy bunch garnering experience and graduate school educations.

Merit. It's kind of a funny, slippery buzzword. Like *accountability*, it seems to imply that public education as it exists today is a feeding trough lined with gluttonous pigs consuming the taxpayers' hard-earned money in a lawless feeding frenzy. There is a chance I could be convinced there's merit to merit-based pay if someone could ever clearly explain to me what merits additional merit-based pay. Crystal clear, right? Let me try again: Exactly what would a teacher have to do to earn some sort of raise? I've only begun to point out the problems with depending too heavily on test scores. What about administrator evaluations? That might work if I could find an administrator whose opinion I valued and respected. With two rare exceptions, my experience with school administrators has been less than favorable. Most of them have been out of the classroom too long. They make more money than teachers but have less contact with students. They make me suspicious by the very nature of having forgone working with students in favor of hitching their wagon to the blob that is the administrative bureaucracy. I was observed by an administrator for a total of 20 minutes over the course of three years before being granted tenure, making it extremely difficult for my district to now get rid of me. Surely I would put a lot of stock into whatever assessment this administrator wrote about me. After all, everything I did as a teacher could be accurately summed up in 20 minutes, just as a child's education can be summed up on a few scan-sheet tests.

No, I don't think merit-based pay will work if the basis for that merit stems from test scores or administrative reviews. What's left? Peer evaluations? That'd be good for morale and collegiality—have teachers criticize one another and fight for raises! Parental evaluations? A good start, I suppose, but first districts would need to shore up parental involvement. When urban schools have to offer meals and ice cream just to get a tiny fraction of parents to attend a function, how carefully would these same parents evaluate their child's teachers?

So, let's see . . . determining a teacher's merit by testing is seriously flawed, by administrative evaluations is simply laughable, by peer evaluation is dangerous, and by parental evaluation unrealistic. I can already hear the counterargument, though. If each of these criteria is worthwhile but a little flawed, why not use them in conjunction with one another? A matrix could be created that combines the test scores of a teacher's classes with a rating assigned by their supervising principal, another number given by their department colleagues, yet another from the parents of their students, a popularity rating from the students themselves, and divided by the total number of photocopies made in a year (to encourage conservation of paper). This matrix, as complicated as it sounds on the surface, works to alleviate the concerns I mentioned earlier about using a single criterion to determine merit.

The problem: If it sounds complicated on the surface, imagine what a logistical nightmare it would be beneath the surface.

Instead, I propose an alternative system.

The second week of school a few years back, a round-faced freshman with round, wire-rimmed glasses took advantage of a lapse in class activity and my encouragement of asking questions to ask about something off-topic. Apparently I had somehow given students the impression I was easily distracted.

"Mr. Miller," he began, "why did you go into teaching?" It is a question that comes up a lot, especially when I start a new class and encourage students to ask me what they want to know in order to help build a rapport. I was ready to respond when the kid continued, following up his benign question with, "I mean, it seems so low."

"Excuse me?"

"Well, you know, it seems like there are so many better things you could have done."

Jaws dropped all around the little pig-faced punk, then the eyes turned to me, the unfamiliar teacher, for an early test of how I would respond to personal insult. The boy asking the question was not actually malicious, which was evident by how quickly he turned red when he realized the tone and implication of what he had said. He immediately tried to cover his tracks by clarifying that he meant there were so many other fields that would have paid more. I gave him a little nod and a smile—just enough to comfort him a little but not enough for him to think I completely believed his backpedaling. Then I gave my theory on teacher salaries.

"Here's the thing about teacher pay."

This was the most attention the roomful of hormones and Ritalin had given me at that early point in the year, so I justly responded by throwing my pitch into full-fledged evangelist mode and giving them a performance, not just an explanation.

"People always ask me if I think teachers should get paid more than athletes or actors who get millions of dollars since the work I do is supposed to be so much more important to our lives and well-being. They ask, expecting me to be predictable and say I deserve more than some sports star. My response, though, is a realist's response. As ridiculous as I think some of those salaries are, I realize it's because they're celebrities who bring in at least that much money in ticket sales for the work they do. Adam Sandler wouldn't get twenty million dollars a movie if his movies didn't earn well beyond that amount."

They understood me. This made sense. But they wondered how much longer I was going to babble about a stupid little question.

"So they get the money they'll bring in. School doesn't work that way. We're not a business. We don't produce products that will, in turn, bring in a certain amount of cash to pay all of us teachers according to the demand for what we sell. I'd argue, though, that we do manufacture a product."

A few of them smiled at my enthusiasm for the subject. I suspected the kid was regretting asking the question in the first place. He probably hadn't thought it through very much, if at all, and now he had drawn the focus of the entire room.

"We make you. At least we try to, anyway, make you into good citizens and good employees. That's what matters, you know, that you can leave here and fill jobs and buy lots of stuff and keep this economy rolling. It's proven that there is a correlation between education and later success."

I was certain there were a number of logistical flaws, and I wasn't terribly serious about my plan. I was a little delighted, however, with my impromptu plan to make myself rich unfolding as I spoke.

"What we're trying to do here is to help you go out and be more successful. If I had my way, if I were King of Schools, I would mandate that teachers get (for the product they produced) a percentage of each student's future income."

Half of them laughed; half were bewildered.

"If we, as teachers, did a good job preparing you for a successful life beyond school, then I would gladly take as my just reward a chunk of everything you make. How about one half of one percent?" I asked, not really expecting an answer. I took out a calculator, made up some numbers as I went, and quickly concluded that I could be making well into six figures under my spur-of-the-moment plan. My students, barely beginning jobs for the first time, were not too keen on the prospect of a "Miller Deduction" showing up on every pay stub for the rest of their lives. Perhaps the plan needed a little work. After all, as with any plan for alternative teacher pay, the devil is in the details.

CHAPTER 7

Sour Lemons

P AY NO ATTENTION TO THE STACK OF ESSAYS ON *Romeo and Juliet* to be scored and added to the final grades. Pay no attention to the full docket of staff meetings that will follow this interminable one. Pay no attention to the plans to be made for a whole new term to begin on Monday. Instead, sit in the lunchroom. Sit contorted, trying to work at the table facing one direction while feigning interest in the faculty speaker behind you. Pay no attention to anything that seems important. Instead, pay attention to the lemon in front of you.

The lemon is more important than grades. It's more important than knowing what to do with a fresh crop of students. Touch it. Get to know it. Learn to recognize your specific lemon even after it has been returned to the table up by the podium and reunited with a pile of nearly identical lemons. This is the answer. Apparently the key to unlocking the mysteries of diversity in the suburban public education system is all here, now, in this lemon. We only need to distinguish one seemingly identical lemon from another. When that skill is mastered, learn to recognize one black kid from another. You mean they're not all the same? Well, thank goodness this lemon came along.

Pay no attention to the stack of essays. There is only your precious lemon. It's not just yellow; it's yellow with a hint of green at one tip. Now you're culturally sensitive.

A common view of diversity in the schools is that there are multiple races or ethnicities represented. Even in a seemingly homogenous white school, though, there is diversity. There is diversity in social status, diversity in interests and talents, and diversity in academic ability. This is the kind of diversity my small-town school experienced in the shadows of the big Twin Cities until recently. As urban sprawl continues, the quaint town at the southern perimeter of the suburbs is exploding exponentially. With the influx of new residents, a more racially diverse population is taking shape. The transformation within the school community has been enlightening to witness. For example, I had been living under the naive assumption that true racists were middle-aged or older—that younger generations were much more open-minded than their parents and grandparents. That's what I used to think. Now I can hardly go into a school restroom without seeing *KKK* or *Kill all niggers* scribbled somewhere on the walls.

About the same time I started teaching at at my present position, the administration decided that it was time for a Diversity Club. All that was needed was a supervisor. As luck would have it, the same year I was hired, the school's only black teacher was hired. The administration couldn't have been happier with itself. They had a clear choice for the diversity coordinator. The fact that they *assumed* the only black teacher would want to be a diversity coordinator, combined with their apparent contentment about having washed their hands of race issues by starting a club, gave me the general impression that matters relating to race, racism, and diversity were not going to be taken seriously.

Oh, as an update, I'm happy to report that nine years later our school has *two* black teachers. Our principal, in a meeting with a teacher he has just hired, refers to two other faculty members not by name, but as "the Hispanic and the Afro-American." And the bathroom graffiti has expanded from racist tirades to include accusations of someone or other being gay and the mandatory homage to smoking pot. The powers that be are trying to cope with the problem by painting the bathrooms darker and darker colors, with the idea that eventually no writing will show up and kids will quit.

The racism that I had hoped was dying out with upcoming generations seems to have adapted, like a mutating virus, and has only *appeared* to vanish. Instead, it's finding new ways of hiding further beneath the surface. We have succeeded in teaching kids that society believes racism is wrong; we have failed to teach our kids not to be racist. They know to be secretive about their hate, lest the righteous teacher comes along and tells them to "be more open-minded."

What can schools do about this, you ask? It's a valid question. Well, as an English teacher, one of the tools at my disposal is using literature to see new perspectives. So far, the results have been less than ideal. Reading Lorraine Hansberry's *A Raisin in the Sun* is boring, kids will say, because all they do is talk. True, most plays don't have car chases or shoot-outs. Reading the excerpt from *The Autobiography of Malcolm X*, when he writes about the literal and figurative pain associated with trying to assimilate his hairstyle to match white people's hair, leads students to the conclusion that "it must suck to have hair like that." We read Harper Lee's *To Kill a Mockingbird*, which I happen to think is valuable on many levels, but we're finally getting sophisticated enough to realize that it does very little to add new perspectives to racial sensitivity. It is, after all, a book by a white author with white protagonists who try (and fail) to come to the salvation of defenseless and stereotypical black characters.

Then again, many of our minority students do little to dispel stereotypes. Self-imposed segregation is the norm. Black boys who would rather be seen as tough than smart sleep through class and strut through the halls. Black girls get into the most vicious exchanges of verbal whippings I have ever witnessed. One young black girl happily alters the popular expression "crack is whack" into "crack is black." One boy of Indian descent welcomes the nickname "Hindu" given to him by his WASP friends.

It's hard even to begin to comment on what I see, because who am I to say it? Who needs opinions on race from another middle-class white man? I'm not sure, but I'm telling anyone who wants to know. There are too many of us in this situation to dismiss the issues. We can't avoid trying to take part in the dialogue just because we don't feel we have a right to.

We have a school full of people who don't know what to do with each other. If a black student behaves like most other students, then everything's fine. If black students have a distinct identity and unique mannerisms, we white teachers start to get uneasy. It's not out of blatant racism. It's out of fear of any responses that could possibly be perceived as racist. What happens when you try to comment on the excessive volume two girls use to talk to one another in the middle of class? Is it classroom management, pure and simple, or is it cultural insensitivity? What if they're the only two black kids in an entire class? Can it still be an objective comment on behavior, or are racist undertones automatically associated?

This fear fuels a sad by-product of not having addressed race matters directly. If equality is what we're striving for, we're not achieving it. Race makes me think twice about whom I call on to give an answer, about whether I stop to ask students if they have hall passes, about how much grief I'll give a student who fails to turn in an assignment. It is quite possible, through my fear of offending any minority students, that I am failing them by being too gentle and not setting the same high expectations I would for anyone else. My effort to avoid singling anyone out has backfired and resulted in exclusion.

And so what do I do? I teach *To Kill a Mockingbird*. It's a book I love, but, as I already mentioned, it's problematic as a tool to combat racism. After all, it's a book in which all but two of the black characters are illiterate.

We do have one text, though, that I teach with great passion because I believe it does have the power to alter souls as well as open eyes. It can make students see beyond their own worlds, just as it made me see beyond mine. It is one of *those* books—the kind that lingers in the back of your mind for the rest of your life, sometimes reappearing when you least expect it and insisting on affecting the direction of your life. It is Elie Wiesel's *Night*. Every student in our school will read the razor sharp, firsthand account of the Holocaust in the autumn of his or her sophomore year. It does not directly address matters of racism in the modern United States, but I have yet to read a more moving testament to the destructive power of hate and the need to treat *all* of humanity *with* humanity. I make every effort to teach the book not only in historical context but from modern relevance, as well. We discuss all the ways in which labeling a population as "other" dehumanizes them, allowing aggressors to act in ways they might not otherwise. We discuss continuing occurrences of genocide around the world. Finally, I think, I'm making a difference.

Then Chris turns in his literary analysis essay. A host of options were at Chris's feet when he was assigned this essay. Most of the possible topics focused on Wiesel's use of literary devices, such as fore-shadowing, imagery, metaphor, repetition, and so on. Chris didn't choose any of these. Chris chose to write a single-paged tirade against Elie Wiesel, the book, and the requirement that led to him reading the book (though I doubt he actually did). His paper, in summary, called Elie Wiesel a whiner for not being able to forget about and get over his time in the concentration camps, accused Wiesel of not being grateful enough that the United States saved him and stopped the war, and said the pain Wiesel experienced was about the same as the pain of being forced to read his book. All 109 pages of it. He went on to ask Wiesel what he thinks should happen to Jews for killing the son of God. Then, as a final confounding statement, the paper concluded with a sentence in all-capital letters reading, "AMERICA, LOVE IT OR LEAVE IT!"

I read Chris's paper five times wondering how I had gone so wrong. What class was this guy in? What class was I in? I wanted to cry. I wanted to hit Chris. I wanted to scream at him as I pounded on him, and then I felt horrid guilt for having such violent thoughts in light of the context. Had I learned nothing from Wiesel? It was time for a new term to begin by the time I had read Chris's paper, so he was already on his way to a new teacher. Not only did I feel like a colossal failure, but he was gone. Perhaps it would be unrealistic to expect I could undo what were probably years of learned bigotry and narrow-mindedness. As unrealistic as it may have been, though, teaching acceptance and humanity was my goal. As blind as I may have been, I thought I was succeeding. For all I know, I may have succeeded with every other student. Every other student may have left my class with a heightened awareness, a greater sense of urgency to combat hatred in all its forms. That might have happened, but I don't know. I do know that, despite my best efforts, Chris left my class unchanged. He left unchanged, but I was more discouraged than ever.

Much has been made of the cliques students form in schools. The rivalry between popular athletes and the counterculture du jour goes back decades. Kids coping with bullying and not fitting in by killing others have shone a bright, if fleeting, light on the need to better understand the dynamics of student social interaction. Fortunately, the severe cases of bullying and the drastic retaliations are fairly rare. Unfortunately, the more cancerous forms of general disrespect and psychological abuse still thrive, flying under the radar of public awareness.

I frequently find myself at odds with students over what is and is not acceptable interaction. The nature of the adolescent personality tends to limit empathy and the ability to imagine consequences beyond their immediate experiences. I have my own experience as a student combined with all I have observed as a teacher. The students have only the experience still unfolding before their eyes without the benefits of distance and perspective.

For example, I face an annual battle every fall to convince kids I'm not an old curmudgeon just because I disapprove of one of their cherished traditions. The school's student council sponsors a week of themed days leading up to the homecoming football game. "Spirit Week" consists of such rousing days as Comfy Day, Hat Day, and Dress-Up Day, among others. The bone of contention comes the final day—Friday—the day of the actual homecoming game. It is Irish Day, because we are the Irish, but in years past the day had a different focus.

The Friday of homecoming week used to be known as Color Day. Students in each grade dressed in a specific color, supposedly in an effort to show school spirit. Instead, freshmen dressed in yellow and sophomores dressed in red became targets for juniors in blue and seniors in green to establish their superiority. They literally mark their territory, as if they are a kind of dog, by branding underclass-men with their color using whatever means available. A freshman may walk into my room after lunch with a green permanent marker streak across his arm, a shot of blue hair spray across his scalp, and a packet of red ketchup smeared across his shirt. Small incidents that smack of hazing and mob mentality running unchecked pop up throughout the day. My colleagues shake their heads and hope we escape the day without anyone getting hurt. In my paranoia, I constantly see the thin line separating fun and games from catastrophe. In their invincibility, the kids see only rites of passage earned and cherished.

A tiny 15-year-old girl, sweet as can be but maybe a little awkward, approaches you with genuine fear in her eyes. "Will they really do all those things I hear about tomorrow?" she asks in a nervous whisper. "Will they know I'm a freshman, even if I don't wear yellow?" Listen to the fear in her voice and just try to convince me that it's only a silly tradition—fun and games and school spirit and all that other bullshit.

Yeah, we're doing fine. We've got respecting a diverse community all figured out. We've got our two black teachers, grade-level warfare, and a bowlful of lemons.

CHAPTER 8

Evolution of a Counselor

JAMES COULDN'T STOP HIMSELF FROM CHANGING INTO A MAD SCIENTIST, so he did his best to halt the metamorphosis by climbing a table and hurling his body against a two-story window in the library's computer lab. He bounced off the glass, fell to the ground, and decided to try again. I sometimes wonder what I would have done had I been there, but as it happened I was not there. James was with his science class. Surrounded by a teacher and classmates who had known him for only a few weeks, it shouldn't be any surprise that the roomful of amused 14- and 15-year-olds giggled and the teacher's jaw dropped. Sensitivity not being the strong suit of most adolescent boys, the following days brought lots of reenactments, with boys chortling, "Look at me, I'm James!" before leaping into the nearest wall or bank of lockers.

I saw James two days later when he returned to school. I asked him how he was feeling, and he replied by telling me he was feeling better now. "The voices kept telling me I was turning into a mad scientist," he continued. "I couldn't stop changing, so I tried to go through the window."

We continued walking down the hall. An opportunity, it seemed. A chance to make a connection. Clearly James was comfortable being candid with me, and I had a sincere interest in at least attempting to be of some use to him. I had no particular reason to want to help James any more than any other student, except that he stood out from his peers as a true individual. He was one of those rare kids who always seemed to be thinking. Oftentimes it seemed he was even thinking about class, about what I was saying, but then again, what do I know? The point is, it *seemed* to me that he was with me—he caught my lame jokes that had only a tenuous connection to the topic at hand. He seemed perceptive and creative. It turns out he was both of those things, but much more than that too. I had no idea what wrestling was going on in his brain: neurons malfunctioning in ways well beyond my comprehension.

I may not have known what was going on in his head, but I seized the opportunity anyway.

"Let me know if you ever want to talk," I muttered with half of a reassuring smile before we parted ways.

"Thanks," he replied absently before wandering off without looking back.

As I continued on to my own room, a recognizable sinking feeling returned. I couldn't quite place it at first, but looking back now, it was clearly the question that plagues me over nearly everything I do at work: why me? Why was I offering to help? I didn't recognize the question as I turned the key to unlock my door, but I recognized the uncertainty of wondering if and when I'd be taken up on my offer to help. Help. A kid tried to throw himself through a window—twice—and I thought I could help. I was going to help him. I swear, I've really got a hubris problem some days.

Even the hardest cynic—I mean, even harder than me—has to acknowledge the grace with which students today conduct themselves in the face of tragedy. A facet of these kids buried deep within them, which I didn't know they had (and they might not even know they had), emerges with grace and maturity when the foundation of their community gets shaken. The school is a community too. With nearly 2,000 students and a couple hundred faculty and staff, the lives that share more waking hours in our building than with their own families are indeed a community bigger than a lot of towns.

Given the size of our population, which is about average for a suburban Minnesota high school, something tragic will happen with some regularity. I sat with my jaw dropped to my desk watching the events of 9/11 unfold. Fourteen-year-old kids I hadn't even known for two weeks entered the room and quickly grasped the gravity of the moment with a casual glance to the TV that turned into a trancelike gaze. They exhibited the epitome of compassion and respect for one another's feelings, almost to the point that I might have wondered where this humanity hid every other day of the week.

Fatal car wrecks occur with freakish consistency: once every other year. On the off years, someone's house will burn down, a parent will die, a senior will be diagnosed with cancer, and, not quite as consistently but still too often, someone will commit suicide.

One cold Wednesday morning, on a day when I was beginning to catch a cold and had given serious thought to calling in sick, a young boy came to my room a little early for first hour.

"There was a really bad accident," he told me. "Lots of cars."

"Really?" I asked, more to acknowledge his statement than to encourage him.

"There'll probably be a lot of people late."

Sure enough, a school-wide email was sent out letting everyone know that a major road near school had been shut down owing to a serious crash and to anticipate late arrivals to class. I didn't say anything to anyone, but I know other teachers were thinking the same thing. If the whole road was being closed off, it couldn't be good.

At 6:44 AM a senior boy was driving to school with his younger brother when he lost control of his car, most likely owed to slushy conditions, and slid across the median into oncoming traffic. Bouncing off the pickup truck would have been bad enough, but not serious. After bouncing off the truck, though, they ended up in the direct path of an oncoming school bus with no time for the driver to react. Did this boy, who earned recognition for both his musical and mathematical skills, who was due to graduate in six months, ever conceive of such an end? What will his younger brother think, over a week later, when he emerges from unconsciousness only to discover that his brother is dead?

By the time an official announcement was made, students had already informed one another about the nature of the accident, the color car that had been obliterated, the names of those who were missing at school and those not answering their cell phones. Many kids already figured out what had happened, and yet it was an entirely different matter to hear the principal confirm the worst.

I have decided that my least favorite sound in the world is not actually a sound at all—it's an unnatural absence of sound. I began the walk from the theater, where my technical theater class had been working, back to my classroom. The passing time between classes and before the first lunch session should have been teeming with energy, buzzing with the ferocity of an angry mob of bees protecting their queen and hive from a delinquent with a slingshot. Instead, the only sounds I could perceive were faint and muted, like holding my head underwater and trying to distinguish the rushing pressure in my ears from the clatter above the surface. The silence of walking down an empty hallway can be disconcerting enough because of its unfamiliarity, but walking through huddles of students with the blank stares of stunned fish feels as unnatural as any other sensory experience I know.

Youth equals life and vitality, and even though I spend much of my days trying to reign it in, the boisterous energy of my students feeds my own energy. To see them jolted to silence jolts me. Sudden, unexpected loss is traumatic for anyone. Certainly the naive sense of immortality most teenagers possess is unrealistic and potentially even dangerous, but that doesn't mean I want to bear witness to the death of their illusions of safety. But what can one expect when so many teenagers spend so much time together? Problems are inevitable. I should have expected it, and yet the subject never came up when I was having parts of speech drilled into my head and hearing about the virtues of proximity as a classroom management tool in my teacher-training classes. Technically my job title says that I teach English, but there hasn't ever been a day in my young career when English was the only matter at hand. It might have been good to know that beforehand. Then again, maybe one simply has to experience it to understand it.

I had already experienced it once a few years earlier, but that didn't leave me any better prepared to deal with adolescent grief in all its raw cruelty in this case. The last time around began with a cryptic voice mail message. One night when I got home, a message from the director of special education simply stated, "The emergency telephone tree has been activated. There is an all-staff emergency meeting in the performing arts center at seven tomorrow morning." The intentionally vague wording of the message, combined with the unusually expressionless voice of the woman I knew normally to be brimming with energy, set all sorts of imagined scenarios into motion.

I couldn't have guessed. I walked in the front door the next morning unprepared for what I saw before me: small clusters of students in various pockets of the halls, standing in circles and crying in one another's arms. Newly arriving freshmen stepped off the bus, into the halls, and stood openmouthed in confusion. Apparently I was not the only one still in the dark. I quickly dropped off my bag and coat in my room and headed down to the meeting for the official word.

Our principal was a wimpy, soft-spoken man, so his attempt to conduct a meeting in a solemn tone made this morning's emergency staff assembly sound disturbingly like any other. He was straightforward and efficiently so. He read to us from the sheriff's department press release about how a county worker driving along a stretch of desolate roadway last night stopped to check on a parked car on the shoulder, at which time he discovered the bodies of two of our students. All evidence indicated a double suicide by self-inflicted gunshot wounds. I strained to hear the names. Ah, selfish relief. Neither of them was familiar to me, and I was free to ponder how rarely one hears about a double suicide. To me the very word *suicide* carries a connotation of isolation. I heard teachers around me gasp and whisper words of disbelief while others murmured explanations to one another that the two kids were a couple, having dated for at least a few months. It suddenly dawned on me that one of the names was familiar after all. Not completely, but the last name. I had the girl's younger brother in a ninth-grade English class.

My mind suddenly raced through every encounter with him throughout the year, and I realized there was importance in an early personal narrative he'd written last fall. How did it go? The boy's mother died, and he went to live with his aunt. Then a year ago (maybe less?), she died too. I strained to recall the details of a paper I read much too hastily one night, but it turned out to be the best I could do. I couldn't remember if he was living with his birth father or in some sort of arrangement with the uncle. Immediately after the meeting, I approached the school psychologist, who had spoken to the faculty about adolescents and the grieving process, and I asked him about the younger brother. He didn't expect the boy to be in school that day, but he suggested that I offer to talk to him if I felt I had a good relationship with him.

Drifting down the hallway, the school was submerged in an eerie silence. I was used to the oppressive quiet at night, when I had worked in the theater well past the last night custodian, but never before had I experienced that quiet in the midst of a crowded hall. I scanned from side to side, taking in images of students grieving, others still confused, as I continued to float. My one lucid thought was that the experience at that moment—that second—was like watching a muted television. I had just been informed of a tragic loss, I knew one of my students was in pain, and I felt like I was watching TV.

As it turned out, the boy *was* in school. He was a quiet young man with an awkward smile and eyes that tugged downward slightly at the outside corners. Thinking I was being the good teacher, I walked into his first-hour class before it began and offered my support in any way I could. I suggested that he feel free to come to my room throughout the morning, especially during the first two hours when I didn't have any other classes in the room. He quietly nodded and thanked me, and I returned to my own room across the hall content that I had done what I could, even though my offer was no more sincere than a neighbor's offer to ask for help anytime. By the end of first hour, stray ninth-grade girls, all of whom I knew, began appearing in my room. They said the boy was coming and had told them all to join him in my room. Students in general were being given great leniency that day to seek out grief counseling as needed, so I thought nothing of having the boy and some of his closer friends come to my room to talk with some privacy.

With second hour underway, I quietly considered the odd assembly across the room from me. The boy had surrounded himself with his closest friends, all girls who were somewhat odd in their own ways: some odd in appearance, others odd in behavior. I alternated between direct involvement in their conversation and hovering at the perimeter while they talked. One girl complained about her mother not letting her answer the phone the night before when another friend called with the news of the deaths. The anger and solemnity over that subject instantly turned to laughter when others pointed out the reason the girl couldn't answer the phone was because she was grounded for not keeping her room clean.

Group laughter turned again to grave matters as another girl started to ask the boy for details. Unsure of myself and at what point, if any, I ought to intervene, I simply listened with apprehensive curiosity. The two were a tumultuous couple; he was a senior and she a junior. Apparently they had been planning the double suicide for some time. It was supposed to take place over the weekend, the boy told his circle of friends and me, but his sister went out with friends instead. The boyfriend was furious. He tore into her over the phone for backing out of their plans. He insisted they follow through with the plan as soon as possible. As soon as possible turned out to be after school that Monday. They both went to school that day. She went on a field trip and had, by all accounts, a great time. The boyfriend was solving mathematical formulaic problems years beyond my comprehension as recently as a half hour before pulling the trigger.

As quickly as the laughter had subsided, it began again. I grew increasingly uneasy. This group could not be reacting in a healthy way, but I wasn't equipped with the skills to lead them in a more meaningful direction. The boy confessed that he didn't do enough to stop her; he saw her writing the note she planned to leave behind Sunday night and didn't say anything to anyone until Monday afternoon. The guilt he felt was quickly dismissed by his friends, none of whom seemed capable of staying serious for any sustained amount of time. His feeling of guilt was an unpleasant subject. Apparently it was okay to discuss unpleasant subjects when *they* wanted to explore them, but not when the person in greatest need wanted to.

I mentioned my surprise to find out that he was in school that day. His response, through those glassy, downturned eyes, was that his dad had left before he woke up, and he didn't want to be home alone. His choice was to stay home alone indefinitely or come to school. Small wonder the family was disintegrating. As I was in the process of reassuring him that he wouldn't have to take an afternoon test he suddenly became worried about, his friends raised the subject of the act itself. They wanted more details. The boy seemed happy to oblige. He went with his father to identify his sister; he should know the gory details they sought. They wanted to know where they held the gun when they shot themselves. In the mouth? Under the chin? At the temple? Which one went first? Which one of them watched the other first before committing the act on their own? How did they know it was a double suicide and not a murder-suicide?

They joked amongst themselves, the boy laughing as much as the rest, about their curiosity and questions being inappropriate. At least one girl showed physical signs of disapproval, while the others innocently looked on for more insight. I felt light-headed. I was beginning to float in my own classroom, much as I had down the hallway. A certain conscious detachment, some sort of defense mechanism, kicked in and muffled the conversation taking place before me. They sounded as though they were at the far end of a damp tunnel, and yet these could very well have been questions in my own head.

Then I heard it—a sign that the boy had had enough. It was small and quiet, but he looked down at his desk and muttered, "You guys..." I knew at that point I had to say something.

Clumsily I blurted out, "I don't think I want to hear any more of this," with a friendly half smile. As if on cue, the boy's counselor suddenly showed up at the classroom door with his pastor. The two went off together, the counselor thanked the boy's friends and me for offering support, and the hour was over. The girls, in various states of melancholy and goofiness, collected their things and ventured off to the rest of the morning. I sat at my desk and shook my head. I held my head in my hands, elbows on the desk, and wished I could lock the door and leave the next class in the hall.

You might think, after this brutal lesson in the importance of minding my own business, I would know better than to freely offer my help again without having any idea where it might lead me. Too late now, though. I had gone and done it again with James after his mad-scientist transformation episode.

Two years later James is in three of my classes and working with me after school. I feel an affinity toward his company. I am drawn to his bizarre imagination, the childlike innocence of his fascination with *Star Wars*, and the inappropriate blurting out of sexual comments (such as when he typed *cock and balls* on a computer and had the automated voice recite the words repeatedly in class).

I have built up enough of a rapport with James that he feels comfortable coming to me to discuss what's on his mind. He once tracked me down after school to tell me about a pressing concern. Other parents in his neighborhood were recently overheard at a party saying that James "belonged in a hospital or locked up." Part of the limitations James has to cope with as a result of his condition is that he's prone to obsessing over matters. He obsesses to a point of no return, where some sort of action becomes necessary despite consequences or expectations. A year ago his need to be near a girl he decided he couldn't live without caused him to jump to his feet in the middle of a class and sprint to another school a few miles away. His proclamations of love fell on deaf ears in the girl's middle-school class. It was her parents, in their seemingly protective instincts, who made the comments at the party.

I listened to James express his frustration. We sat together in the back of the theater, where I could keep a watchful eye on my techies down on the stage as they built the set for the current play.

"I want to say something to them. I want them to know that's not who I am," he told me.

"That's understandable," I replied, when what I was thinking was more along the lines of, *Don't go near them! You really are crazy if you think approaching them is a good idea!*

The problem was compounded by a scheduling oversight that now landed James and the girl, now a freshman, in the same class at the same time—my class. There was a strict understanding, at the request of the girl's parents, that their schedules shouldn't cross, and yet there they were.

"I've been working really hard to do what I'm supposed to."

"You have, and people have noticed." People *had* noticed. Other than a streaking incident at a pep fest that thankfully wasn't seen all the way through to fruition, James had been having a relatively tame year.

"What should I do?"

Several tech kids down on the stage were gathering around a platform, apparently discussing how to figure out the angles to connect it to another platform. They glanced up at me occasionally, aware that I probably shouldn't be disturbed, but spinning their wheels until I could come help. James sat next to me sheepishly waiting for some sort of guidance. It was the opportunity to help I was imagining when I first offered to talk, and a year and a half later I finally felt like I was helping in a concrete way.

"Well, I know you want to say something to these people, but do you think they'd really listen?"

"No."

"You have been working hard, and I think the best thing you can do is to let them see that. You have an opportunity here, because of the class you're both in, to show them there's nothing to worry about."

"Yeah."

"I know it doesn't do anything about how you feel right now, but I think it's your best chance to change their minds. Show them through your actions rather than just talk."

"Okay," James muttered and stood to leave.

"You're feeling better?" I asked, happy to have helped but still just a little nervous about where he'd go from here.

"Yeah."

"What are you going to do now?"

"Well, I'll probably go home, let my dog lick my face for three or four minutes, have a bowl of cereal, and read for twenty minutes."

"Okay. I'll see you tomorrow." His specificity was unusual but reassuring. That was his plan, and I doubted he would stray from it. He left without another word or glance. I watched him leave, feeling a rare sense of personal satisfaction. Maybe offering to help isn't a hubris problem, after all. Maybe being available to listen is enough. James left the family alone and, by all evidence, got over the comments he had heard. At the time I felt I had actually made a difference, and it didn't hurt a bit. I lingered in the back row of seats for a moment after James left, but before long the techies noticed I was free and called for some assistance. One good deed done, I returned to the stage to ponder angles with all my other kids.

While I feel like I have a hubris problem sometimes, there are plenty of other days when reality cuts me back down to size in a hurry.

James continued to take my classes throughout the next year, but he struggled. His energy dropped off tremendously, but so did his outbursts and anxiety. It appeared to be an unfortunate side effect of the medication he was taking. I overlooked a lot more behavior than I should have. I can claim I truly thought it was the medication, and there may be some truth to that, but there was probably some vanity at play too. Looking back, I can see that I relished James's admiration so much that I became blind to his continuing problems.

I ran into James's mother early one morning in the hallway as she spoke to another teacher. I greeted her cheerfully only to be met with a sober hello, her eyes red with tears.

"You should know this too," she began. "James was hospitalized over the weekend for an overdose. We're working on getting him into rehab."

I stood speechless as I mentally connected all the dots that seemed so obvious in hindsight. I realized I had become part of the cliché, part of the population that "failed to act on the clear warning signs" or something along those lines. I could almost hear myself being chastised by an investigative reporter, maybe Geraldo Rivera, in melodramatic tones. Of course the lethargy, the half-closed eyes, the bizarre ramblings were signs of drug use. How could I not see that?

I paused mid-sentence during James's class every time I glanced at his empty desk while he was hospitalized. For six weeks he received intensive addiction therapy, mental health therapy for obsessive-compulsive disorder, and physical therapy for the extensive liver damage the drugs had caused—particularly the inhalant abuse.

I am not a trained counselor, but many times I feel I ought to be. If I want to really be of service to these broken kids, maybe a background in counseling would be apropos. My role as counselor troubles me, though. Not because it is uncomfortable or because I don't want to help. I am not troubled by the time or emotional investment. I am troubled by the importance of getting it right—the high stakes of these kids' lives—and my own insecurities. I continue to believe it is best to do what I can in spite of my possible shortcomings, but it is terribly difficult to silence that nagging inner voice whispering, "Drop it . . . other people can deal with this better than you . . . move on . . . it's not your problem."

Yet I frequently find myself in that precarious position of mentor, counselor, or role model. Sooner or later, I suppose, I'll either screw up so badly I'll never make personal connections with kids again, or I will get comfortable enough with myself and my intuition that the doubts and anxiety will fade. One can hope it's the latter. Until then, wish me luck.

CHAPTER 9

Sisyphus and the Research Paper

OT ALL OF THE TRIAL AND TRIBULATIONS OF TEACH-
ING HIGH SCHOOL ENGLISH are as obvious and dramatic
as a death threat. The mundane irritants, like water drop-
lets boring a hole through a rock, can do just as much harm. Simplistic thinking and writing full of errors, caused by the mutual efforts
of carelessness and ignorance, plague me as a teacher. It's why I'm so
reluctant to begin grading essays after collecting them. I begin to feel
overwhelmed by the task of righting a ship so severely off course.

I love tipping my chair back on its rear legs, resting my feet on the
edge of my desk and adjusting slightly to find a comfortable balance.
I often sit this way while correcting papers. Reading through a pile of
topic proposals from my senior research paper course one day, I noticed
many familiar questions and jotted down many familiar comments:

Should schools have open campus?—*Not an open-ended question.*

Should marijuana be legalized?—*Not an open-ended question.*

How can schools be improved?—*Be more specific.*

What causes serial killers?—*What? What do you expect to be able to say about this? Where is the controversy?*

Then I saw it—the one that set me off. Two days into the term Gina had already demonstrated a substantial lack of motivation, restraint, and respect. I had decided I didn't like her, something teachers aren't supposed to do.

Beauty school.—*This is not a question or an evaluative research paper topic.*

I returned the papers the next day, and five minutes later I saw the wiggly eyes and roly-poly face of Gina hovering over me at my desk with a goofy, snaggletooth smile.

"I don't get it, Mr. Miller. What's wrong with this?"

"Well, it's not a question . . . right?" I asked after a momentary pause as I became uncertain of whether or not she was aware that those two words did not comprise a sentence.

"Right," she finally conceded.

"So the first thing you need to do is make sure that what you write is a question. Then . . . what do beauty schools have to do with the kinds of topics you can use in this class? You need a social issue and you need to be able to provide your resolution to the issue, which you then support with your research."

"Uh-huh." I had lost her.

"It's almost like the persuasive speeches you did in ninth and tenth grades, only it's all about the research and not so much about what you personally think.

"Um, so how do I use beauty schools?" Her goofy smile was long-gone. She had a forlorn look as she waited for me to provide an answer.

"I don't know. That's why I wrote you that comment. It may be possible, there may be some way, but I don't know what it is off the top of my head."

In the opening chapters, I described the schools as full of broken kids. Despite the many inspirational exceptions to this pessimistic generalization, there is one trend that simply cannot be ignored. My colleagues and I are hyperaware of it, but the matter crosses over all subjects. Reading is work. Writing is work. In a culture of more fun, more convenience, and more instant gratification, kids have a hard time buying into the notion of work paying off. Why read a book when watching the movie is easier, faster, and more fun? Why revise a paper when it's already been typed and spell-checked?

Of all the problems facing schools—and there are some monumental ones out there—the most pressing has got to be students who just don't see school as worth the effort. Again, not every kid, but many students go through the motions daily, waiting out their perceived incarceration, putting the minimum effort required to keep teachers and parents off their backs. In cases where parents will ride the kids until grades are up, there are many success stories. In cases where parents don't even know their child's grades let alone stress the importance of excelling, there are many tragic failures. As teachers we like to remind anyone who will listen of the role family plays in a child's attitude and effort. Parents who model valuing education will likely find themselves with children who value education. Parents who devalue education, either explicitly or through indifference, will find themselves with children needing outside influence to develop a mind-set that values the pursuit of knowledge in the traditional academic sense.

The problem with remaining focused on the role of family, as teachers, is that at best we run the risk of hand-wringing too much over something we can't control or, at worst, dismissing students as lost causes. I cannot speak for my counterparts at the elementary- or middle-school levels, but at the high school level there is a strong sense of desperation that an inexact (yet substantial) portion of our students' personalities, ethics, and values have been formed before we even meet them. That's not to say kids don't change during high school—quite the contrary—rather they are far from the relatively blank slates I imagine them to be as young children. Each year of schooling, each year of learning or not learning, has a cumulative effect that becomes more difficult to influence by the late teens.

What then to do about the kids with learned helplessness? Who turn to me in frustration when I ask them to develop an original idea for a paper topic and instead plead with me to just assign one? In the monotony and demands of daily teaching, I have little patience for these needs. Rather than nobly trying to lift each kid up, as I catch myself implying teachers ought to do in the preceding paragraphs, I fall into one of two traps. Depending on circumstances, I may either leave them to fend for themselves in a sink-or-swim mentality, or I may actually succumb to the even more destructive approach of giving them what they ask for. I just might assign the topic for the girl who can't develop her own. I just might give an extra day for a homework assignment because some verbally gifted kids in the front row convinced me that half the class not finishing the work is proof the deadline was unreasonable.

Dr. David Walsh has published some remarkable work in this area, including his thought-provoking work *No: Why Kids—of All Ages—Need to Hear It and Ways Parents Can Say It.* I saw Dr. Walsh speak during teacher workshops one August before the start of another school year, and I was struck by the parallels between his comments on parenting and my work as a teacher. Many of us complain about the parents who enable their kids, like the mom who pleads with a teacher to allow late work to be accepted (as my mother kindly did for me), but it occurred to me that we as teachers are just as guilty. It was jarring to see the obvious connection between giving my daughter candy to placate her before a tantrum ensued and scaling back expectations on a class assignment because of students complaining about the rigor involved. I could not excuse myself from complicity just because I was a teacher who had no control over my students' families. We all had a hand in the educational culture we find ourselves in. Then again, standing my ground wasn't necessarily a gratifying experience, such as with Gina.

I never thought I would miss that stupid grin and the ridiculous "yuk-yuk" voice that went with it, but during the following two months I began to realize it was better than Gina's whining, do-this-for-me tendencies that I now had to live with daily. I baby-stepped her through the process of choosing a topic, a difficult task since she swore she had no interests in anything and the one possibility related to beauty schools I was able to come up with for her wasn't good enough, she decided. One afternoon, weeks into the term and sitting safely within my fortress of solitude (a desk, table, and three file cabinets carefully arranged in a corner), I looked up from my stack of papers to see Gina actually close to tears as she stood across from me.

"Why are you so mean to me?" Gina was whining again.

"What's wrong?" I was, admittedly, more interested in how she was implicating me in some self-induced trauma than how I might be able to help her.

"You got me in trouble. You called my mom and now she's mad at me."

"I got you in trouble? You're the one who hasn't written a paper yet," I retorted. "I was simply answering her questions about how you were doing in here."

"I'm going to get kicked out now."

"I'm sure you won't get kicked out over a paper," I muttered. What I was really thinking was the exact same thought I had every day. It haunted me daily from exactly 10:19 AM to 11:08 AM: *Why are you here? This is a class specifically geared to the college-bound! You aren't even sure if you can handle beauty school!*

"My mom was real mad!" she bellowed and then began manically laughing and yuk-yukking and flashing the ugly smile.

"Well, if she only talked about kicking you out and didn't actually do it, I guess I didn't say enough bad things about you," I stated briskly and returned to my papers to indicate I was done with the conversation.

Two days later I had Gina removed from class, citing the statistical improbability that she could pass and the distraction she caused for others. She could rot for the last two weeks in transitional study hall: an invention unique to our school—basically a suspension-like purgatory.

"I'm back, Mr. Miller! Are you happy to see me?"

A single, remaining shred of professionalism prevented me from weeping. The many years of growing up in a stoic home came to bear as I masked all emotional responses. My assignment to TSH had been overturned by the principal, and Gina was back in the room. The action was predicated by an irate phone call from her mother, who argued that Gina was "slow" and never received the kind of assistance I ought to have been providing. It was decided, in a meeting I was not invited to, that Gina would receive a grade of "Incomplete" at the end of the term and have at least a month to work with me outside of class to make the paper up.

I tell someone who doesn't teach about irrationally fearing for my life and I get pity that times have gotten so hard. I tell someone that one kid, one research paper, is going to drive me to distraction and they just don't get it. Small wonder I spend my time feeling like I'm teaching in circles.

CHAPTER 10

Open Letters Number 2 and Number 3

T O MY FIRST STUDENTS,

I wasn't much of a teacher for you, I'm afraid. My greatest weakness was my inability to cope when I lost control of you. I didn't have any of the techniques of veteran teachers to rein in talkativeness or defiance. Instead, if you were loud I tried to be louder. If you were rowdy I tried to be rowdier. In my frustration I would behave in a horribly unprofessional manner. Like a toddler who acts out because he can't use words to express anger, I threw chairs and kicked desks—never at any of you, but inexcusably aggressive all the same. I'm calmer now, and I wish you could have had more of the teacher you deserved back then. Of course you weren't really my first students. You were out in the northern reaches of the Twin Cities, in St. Francis, and were kind enough to collect letters from students on my behalf when my position was cut. Your effort was in vain as far as influencing the school board was concerned but heartwarming to a new teacher experiencing his first major career setback.

To my *real* first students,

You are my big secret. I am too ashamed to mention you to anyone when I talk about my years of teaching. It is bad enough that I oftentimes feel like a failure as a teacher. Remembering you makes me feel like both a failure and a quitter. I had just finished student teaching in Minneapolis when I got the call for an immediate job opening at a junior high in St. Paul. A full-time job in the middle of a school year was an opportunity not to be ignored. If only I had known what I was getting myself into.

You were students in need of remedial reading instruction. You had been bounced around from teacher to teacher, none of them with any English/language arts/reading training, and none of them with any curriculum to guide them. I was supposed to be the qualified one who would make a difference. You were overwhelmingly black, poor, and bitter. I was overwhelmingly unprepared, outnumbered, and unhappy. There never should have been so many of you in one class. Kids who are truly behind in reading need low student-teacher ratios. They need individual attention and carefully planned lessons. I stood in the middle of an art room and tried to get 30 of you to read something. Anything. You laughed at me. I tried to call your parents to complain about your behavior, only to find your phone had been disconnected. Every night you went home to places and families I still can't imagine to this day. Every night I went home and drank. I would lie on the couch, hardly able to function. I had been your teacher for eight days when I gave my two-week notice. I crashed and burned. Back then, I found it comforting when I heard my replacement didn't last any longer than I had. Back then, I felt like it was your fault.

CHAPTER 11

Settling

THERE HAVE BEEN TIMES when I am absolutely certain I have made a mistake of epic proportions. I have contemplated what else I could do for a living. I have even applied and interviewed for jobs—everything from technical writing to education programming at a major arts center in St. Paul. I never get offered any of those jobs, which in a sense is a relief because it spares me from having to make an extremely difficult decision.

Even as I would breathe a certain sigh of relief every time an application submitted on a lark led to nothing, I did still see my job at my school as temporary. It was my rebound job, holding me over until the job I really wanted came along, whatever that was. Actually, I did know what that was: a prominent school in a beautiful community with a brand-new building was looking for an English and theater teacher the very summer I had been cut from my first position. The position was posted at the end of the summer, but I had already accepted my school job. Looking out for my best interests, though— since no one else ever does—I pursued the opening. The interviews went well, the school looked great, the administrators seemed supportive, and then the bottom dropped out. In the process of checking my references, the interviewing administrator decided one last step needed to be taken before offering me the job. She decided to check with the principal out of courtesy to ask about releasing me from my newly signed teaching contract. The principal refused.

I pleaded desperately with the administrator when I heard the news and convinced her to hold off on making any final decisions until I had a chance to talk to my new principal. I tried to call him immediately. Teachers break contracts all the time. Even the Human Resources Department told me that I would simply need to submit a letter to resign (but suggested it might be nice to know as soon as possible since school was to start in two weeks). Other principals and administrators I knew all told me that this sort of thing happens all the time—some teachers will come and go up to the last minute of summer. My frantic voice mail left with my principal went unanswered. The other school refused to make an offer without my principal's consent, and so I saw my dream job slip away.

The following Monday morning, when I arrived for the first day of training for teachers new to the building, my principal approached me. The conversation that followed was all he ever said to me my entire first year.

"I got your message this weekend," he said, sheepishly looking at the floor more than me.

"Uh-huh."

"I must have written your number down wrong or something, because I tried to call you back and it didn't work . . . But . . . here you are . . ."

"Yup."

After a brief, awkward silence we turned and walked our separate ways.

That encounter (or lack of an encounter) set the tone for the first year at the school and fostered my wanderlust. I was, I am not ashamed to admit, a bitter and resentful bear that year. All right. I confess that in many ways I still am. It is amazing to me how a person can piss me off so badly that he can never do right by me again. The job was temporary—the rebound job.

My wife Kimberly and I bought our first home, a modest 1950s rambler, in the suburbs just north of Minneapolis–St. Paul. She had been teaching for a year in downtown St. Paul, and I was just hired to teach at the far northern edge of the metro area. Since job security simply doesn't exist as a nontenured teacher, we wanted to be centrally located. Neither of us could be sure what the future would hold.

When I made the move from my last position to my current one, I swapped a 20-mile drive for a 27-mile drive. Fifty-five miles a day. Over an hour of every day of my working life spent in the car, and untold dollars spent on gas that wasn't getting any cheaper over time. The frequent evening events took their toll. On a typical school day, students got out at 2:30 PM and teachers would stay until at least 3:00. Whenever I was working on a play and performances rolled around, I would need to be around to get things started at 5:00. There was never any point in driving home only to turn around and come back. There definitely wasn't any chance of running home between school and parent-teacher conferences in the evening.

Between the commute and other obligations, the extra time spent away from home began to wear on me and, I think it's safe to say on her behalf, it really began to wear on my wife. She is a strong woman, but she is not someone who enjoys being alone. She might call to see how late I was going to be painting whatever set I was building when dinnertime came and went with no sign of me showing up at home, and I would rarely know when I would be leaving. I always offered the best-case scenario, saying something like, "I'll be out of here in half an hour. I'll be home before you go to bed." There would be a slight hesitation, a barely audible sigh, before Kim would reply with the same, "Okay. See you later," which told me she knew I would really be two hours. I cringed whenever I heard that hesitation, and her disappointment motivated me to get the work done even faster, but even finishing up in ten minutes after that meant another hour before I would actually walk in the door of my home.

Remember, the job was temporary. It was the transition to bigger and better things, and so the commute continued. We remodeled more and more of our house, making us more and more attached to our home as we had created it. Then we had our first child. Suddenly being gone so much hurt even worse because precious time with our daughter in her most formative years was spent sitting in traffic or winding through back roads. Passing comments about how nice it would be to live closer to work took on a more serious tone.

The more we considered the option of moving, the more reasons we found to support it. The more it seemed like we would actually move, the more anxious I began to feel. I was finishing my sixth year of my temporary rebound job. Moving to the neighborhood meant facing a harsh reality I had been denying: This job was not temporary. Something better was not about to come along. For the first time,

I wouldn't be able to approach my job with the cavalier attitude that I could just leave if I wasn't happy. As much as the move was going to improve so many aspects of my life, there was a distinct sense of disappointment when I realized that I had peaked professionally at 30 years old.

There is no opportunity for advancement as a teacher. One cannot go from junior teacher to executive vice-presidential teacher. There is simply teacher. Year after year, teacher teacher teacher. Sure, there are some awards along the way. I could try for National Board Certification, but that is little more than a feather in a cap. Granted, it's a very impressive feather, but it does not actually change the job.

My ideas of moving up the academic teaching ladder were to work my way into more and more prestigious schools. I might even pursue postsecondary teaching. There always seemed to be something else just a little bit further on the horizon, but all of it vanished with a sigh of resignation when we moved from our central location where anything was possible to the far southern suburbs, where we cemented the previously unspoken assumption that I would be teaching here for at least the next several years.

In addition to spending less of my life in my car and more at home, the move to my school's community has merged many aspects of my personal and professional life. I now see current and former students at the grocery store. They serve my food at restaurants and pour my beer at the bar. I see parents on the street who recognize me from conferences but whom I am unable to connect to their son or daughter on short notice. When Kim and I explored potential churches to join, one of our key considerations suddenly became which students I recognized. Frankly, there are some I would rather not bump into on a Sunday morning.

I remember a guest speaker at one of our student teaching semi-nars talking about her strategies for improving the quality of schools. A cornerstone of her philosophy was the hardest for me to swallow at the time: teachers should live where they teach. She was sentimental about the days when kids were afraid of their teachers because they knew they would catch hell when teachers ran into parents at the hardware store or at church. Kids had a different view of teachers when there was a chance one might show up for dinner one night. I scoffed at the notion as antiquated and impractical. Besides, I thought, I wanted work to be work and private life to remain private. I liked not having to worry about students showing up on my doorstep, whether they meant well or ill. I sat at that seminar and swore that would never be me.

Ah, the best laid plans.

My skepticism at the time was rooted more in defiance than any philosophical opposition. I simply was not going to let anyone hint that I ought to live by my students and their families. No one was going to tell me where to live. Funny how things like commutes and the feel of a neighborhood don't seem like priorities to a college stu-dent. I can certainly see why people still choose to keep their distance, but I am a changed man when it comes to this subject. It's become a source of amusement for my family to walk up to a store entrance only to hear an excited voice calling from behind us in the parking lot, "Hey! Mr. Miller! Going shopping?" We will turn and look, finding smiling kids leaning out their car windows with giant grins.

It's likely the closest I will come to experiencing celebrity status, and it makes for a great job-stress tonic.

CHAPTER 12

Retreating

PUBLIC SINCERITY AND OPTIMISM normally do not come easily to me. I want good things for my students, yet most are so accustomed to my twisted sense of humor that they would laugh if I came right out and said I cared about them. Sometimes I find this to be a depressing reputation to have earned, but I suspect they know I hope they know. It is not a matter of how they react when they hear me say I care, it's a matter of whether they believe me enough to come when they need me.

All the same, I get sick of myself. Our school lined up a "respect retreat" for every ninth-grade student in the building. Each word by itself—*respect* and *retreat*—would typically make me queasy, but the two combined nearly brought on a bout of diarrhea. The notion that respect could be indoctrinated was absurd, and indoctrination was what I envisioned when I heard that the students would be hauled up to a local church for the day to be guided by a nonprofit organization called Youth Frontiers.

I found the idea laughable when I heard about it, but I was determined to hate the entire experience when teachers were assigned to come along for the ride. Our roles were uncomfortable ones: to be active spectators. We were to make a statement of support by our mere presence while handing over total control to the retreat organizers. It is hard to ask teachers, who typically have had to develop at least a little bit of a control-freak tendency in order to survive in classrooms, to escort students on a field trip only to hang in limbo on the periphery.

Trust me, I have no compulsion to be an on-task kind of person. No one will ever mistake me for a type A personality. All the same, I like to spend my time how I choose and not as an idle hostage to the touchy-feely respect cult. Images flashed before me of every awkward workshop, every humiliating camp, every demeaning team-building event I was ever subjected to. "Oh, good," I thought to myself, "I get to sit through another one."

The retreat was the second day of a new term, and the second day of a new term is always a disastrous time for me. After two long days of final exams, students depart for a three-day weekend while the rest of us convene on a Friday supposedly to close the books on the previous term and submit grades. We also try to coordinate and plan within the department our curricula for upcoming classes. And, of course, we have meetings of great consequence where we do things like acquaint ourselves with a lemon to unravel the mysteries of diversity. Of course, I don't finish and submit my grades, I don't plan the next term's classes, and I'm usually behind schedule on finishing the set for whatever production we're working on at the time. My day to get work done fills with one meeting after another, my stack of ungraded essays remains untouched, and I leave at night more exhausted than I am on a normal teaching day.

When the second day of the next term arrives, so do the messages from the administration about overdue grades. They get progressively nastier the longer I go past the deadline. Is it any wonder I have a difficult time holding a hard line on late work with my students?

On this particular second day of the term—the day of progressively nasty messages—I was certain that for once my to-do list was actually going to kill me. I would sit down at my desk, look over everything, hear a high-pitched sound like a boiling teapot, and suddenly my brain would spew from my ears in a liquefied explosion. The air temperature that December morning was teetering back and forth between single digits above and below zero. I was sleep-deprived from late nights of grading papers and the anticipation of knowing I would soon be even more sleep-deprived with the birth of our second child. Cold, tired, hungry, in despair, I was ready to lash out at the slightest provocation if anyone tried to make me be peppy, happy, or in any way optimistic.

I stood in the church lobby, the first teacher to arrive, waiting for something to happen. Anything. Something worthwhile would have been refreshing, but something worthless would be deliciously vindicating. A woman approached, rushed and out of breath, to ask if I was the administrator in charge. Even though she was probably close to me in age, her piercings, multicolored hair, and effortless bohemian dress made me feel substantially older. Discovering I was not the person she needed, I was abandoned as quickly as I had been found. I stood again, waiting for something to happen.

The herd of students was unloaded from the school bus that had mercifully driven everyone the half mile we were all supposed to have walked. We then stood, some 130 students and a handful of teachers, crammed in the vestibule of the church. Now we were all waiting for something to happen. When something did finally happen, it first appeared to confirm my worst fears: The kids were called into a large assembly room with pop music blaring and group leaders with way too much pep cheering and clapping as each student stepped in. I was in desperate need of coffee. A stiff drink would have been nice, but coffee would have been lifesaving.

All of the expected icebreakers followed—silly activities meant to make everyone feel equally ridiculous and therefore free of inhibitions. Hours of silliness followed. Over 100 kids formed a semblance of a circle and then attempted to simultaneously sit on one another's laps. They played a round of Simon Says. They held a dance-off. Clearly this was a wonderful use of time. I was ready to start walking back to the school myself.

Then the woman sang and the man spoke.

It's always amazing how penetrating music can be—that mystifying way it can speak more directly to the soul than mere words alone. The woman's voice was strong but not overbearing, intense but calming. It blended seamlessly with her acoustic guitar, and, when she sang, 130 15-year-olds were silent and still. I was, in a word, disarmed.

Then the man told a story. He described a horrifying experience at the conclusion of his career as a summer camp director—an incident involving several early-teen girls physically beating and verbally assaulting a campmate on a bathroom floor "for fun." The story itself, though, didn't make nearly as strong of an impression on me as his closing point.

My skepticism was based on the wrong premise. I thought the organizers hoped somehow to make all of these kids suddenly treat each other well, a monumental task among teenagers notorious for ruthlessly cutting each other down. I thought the touchy-feely approach would lead to epic backlashes, causing more trouble than good among a population just as cynical as me. As I watched, however, I saw kids listening intently. They weren't just quiet; they had the serious look of people listening to what they hear while looking deep within themselves. Brows furrowed, heads lowered, tears welling in eyes. They were actually looking into their pasts, mentally reviewing whatever acts of cruelty filled their memories—acts they had either committed or endured.

The point of the day, it turned out, was simply to offer a taste. The kids had an entire day to taste freedom from harassment, to taste fun without fear, to taste complete respect among peers. They listened to the counselors telling horrific stories they could relate to—tales of bullying, bulimia, and suicide—stories that could easily have been about them or their friends. They sat with strangers—classmates they didn't know and seniors who served as small-group leaders—to define what respect looks like and how it shows up in daily life. The theory was, rather than trying to impose respectful behavior, let the kids experience it for themselves and they'd want more. Why not? Samples are used all the time to hook consumers. Why couldn't the same approach work with kids? Give them a daylong taste. Maybe they'll get hooked.

For once, I wanted to believe it would work. I wanted to believe I would see a genuine change in the juvenile cruelty that litters every day I spend with students. I was disgusted with how I had pouted that morning. The effort undertaken by the session leaders was genius in its apparent simplicity and noble for the purity of its intentions. It worked for a day. Kids who couldn't be more disparate laughed together as if restraints had been loosened. If only it could last.

Of course, it doesn't last. Ninth graders are such peculiar beasts. They are mature enough to understand the importance of treating each other well, but what they are able to understand frequently doesn't matter. Make no mistake about it: The metamorphosis from child to burgeoning adult is ugly, violent, and ruthless. Everyone agreed that the respect retreat was worthwhile, everyone wanted to support the creation of a positive and caring environment, and everyone was the same a week later as he or she was before the retreat. Smirking boys chortled whenever a classmate dared to read Romeo with even the slightest hint of inflection or enthusiasm. They stole candy from each other's bags, sometimes as a joke and sometimes simply to steal. These same smirking boys have to be reminded not to snatch hats from each other and then chase each other around the room like ten-year-olds.

The girls are in many ways at a disadvantage. The boys have so successfully lowered everyone's expectations that no one really expects boys to be able to control their behavior. Girls, on the other hand, seem to mature earlier. Glimpses of civilized behavior, combined with the need to counterbalance the boys' behavior, makes many teachers count on ninth-grade girls to be the sane element of the classroom. Nobody wins in this situation, because teachers are eventually disappointed when girls inevitably revert to juvenile behavior. While these girls want to be all grown-up most of the time, they're still 14 or 15, after all. Girls become frustrated when they perceptively detect the ensuing double standard. Boys get away with things girls get called to task for.

Two months later the drama of rowdy boys and moody girls continued to unfold at a dizzying pace, and neither teacher nor student anywhere seemed to spend any time thinking about a polar December day when we all stepped off a bus, passed through the biting wind into a church, found literal and figurative warmth among our peers, and got our one-day taste of a day unencumbered by social anxiety.

I get sick of being cynical sometimes, but then, is it really cynicism if so many of my doubts turn out to be correct?

CHAPTER 13

Toxic Julie

M Y DAUGHTER IS FOUR YEARS OLD. In what I know will be a dizzying leap forward in time, she will someday be the same age as the adolescent girls who fill my classes. Some are sweethearts who would make me a proud father, but far more of them give me premature nightmares.

As a father, fashion scares me. I know trends will change in the next 10 to 12 years, but every so often I see something that simply makes me shake my head. Shaking my head, I catch a glimpse of the framed picture of my little girl next to my desk. I cannot reconcile the scantily clad 14-year-old girl with thong underwear exposed and cleavage bubbling out of low-cut shirts with the image I have when peeking in on my sweetie before leaving for work that morning and seeing how peacefully she sleeps in her head-to-toe fleece pajamas.

As a father, technology scares me. The old-fashioned ideas of perverse uses for a Polaroid camera are nothing compared to what kids can do today with digital images and video. Teenage girls, already obsessing over appearance, can now test the waters to see what kind of model they'd make. The more they want to be glamorous, the more they want to emulate their heroes, the more risqué the pictures. They all have phones that can share these images instantaneously, and many have blogs that reveal far more personal information than the average stranger ought to be able to access with far too racy of images. I hear about this stuff early on compared to most parents, I suspect, because kids in school talk to their friends a little too loudly. I catch comments they would more carefully suppress in the presence of their parents.

As a father, Julie scares me more than any student I have ever met. Julie is 17 and embodies every trait I hope my child shuns. My first experience with Julie occurred the fall of her freshman year. The first day of school, while reviewing course objectives and expectations, she blurted out full volume, "This is so boring!" Hearing comments like that one is not unusual, but one of my favorite reasons for teaching freshmen is the honeymoon period in September, when the kids are still anxious, impressionable, and mostly controlling their behavior until they develop a greater comfort level. Classes that will be boisterous to the point of giving me regular headaches start the fall as quiet and serious as a funeral gathering. Few smile. Even fewer laugh out loud. Volunteers to read or answer questions are hard to come by.

I miss those early days, when all Julie complained about was being bored. Instead, she quickly progressed to violent, profanity-laden tirades at the slightest provocation, such as a glance from another student or my request that she sit in her desk. She was a hideously ugly girl, not so much because of the physical structure of her face, but because of the way she contorted her face grotesquely to show her disdain. She often lowered her head to glare out from under her brows. Her hooked nose was accentuated whenever she lifted her upper lip into an epic sneer, which was more often than not. I was delighted to hand her over to another teacher that year in a move deemed to be in everyone's best interest.

While at least half of my teaching load is freshman English, I always have a smattering of other classes. Sometimes it's tenth-grade English, sometimes theater classes like acting or tech, and sometimes it's a class geared toward seniors, such as research paper, creative writing, or journalism. I never anticipated, when I began teaching, the joy to be found in watching kids grow up. It was a peculiar sensation when I had been here long enough to teach seniors I once had in class as freshmen. I am already at an age when I don't view four years as terribly significant, and to hear my older colleagues speak, time will only slip away with progressively greater speed. Every time I run into a repeat customer, though, I see the monumental difference between a 14-year-old starting high school and an 18-year-old on the verge of graduating and realize four years can make a profound difference. The changes are physical and emotional, intellectual and social. It's usually a delight to witness. The process has all sorts of names, most of them corny ones like *blossoming* or *coming of age*, but it is indeed a metamorphosis that makes me feel like something important is going on in high school. It's as if a product 18 years in the making is getting the final detailing before being released to the general public.

Sometimes, though, the ones you don't want to see again come back. Like Julie.

A new year was underway, and fall classes were going well. I was adjusting to teaching journalism for the first time and was developing a comfort and rapport with my students. Until two weeks into the term, when I received notice that Julie was being added to one of my journalism classes to earn a senior English credit. In the years that had passed since Julie's freshman year, I had learned a lot through other teachers and her friends that helped me understand her better. I found out from her mother that men were generally a problem for her. Men in positions of authority were even worse. I never heard the details, nor did I want to, but my heart sank when I learned this animosity stemmed from having been raped shortly before high school had begun. Her counselor told me her violent mood swings were officially diagnosed as bipolar disorder. Julie's special-education case manager assured me she had been making great progress, so I shouldn't expect a repeat of ninth grade.

Julie chose to sit next to her close friend, which unfortunately was next to my desk in the back of my room. Her friend seemed to me a good kid, but Julie's presence brought out an unfortunate side in her. From this vantage point, Julie had a clear view of the picture of my daughter, and I cringed whenever Julie made a comment about her. I didn't have any kids the first time I met Julie, and this was the first time a student talking about my daughter made me uncomfortable.

"Just wait till she's a teenager, Mr. Miller!" she'd laugh. "What are you gonna do when she gets her tongue pierced like me?" she'd ask and flick her tongue out repeatedly to show the pink stud sticking through her flesh. It always looked like she was eating a mint that refused to disintegrate.

"I'll probably cry," was all I could come up with. I am frequently honest with my classes by simply using an air of sarcasm to mask my sincerity. They might catch on, they might not. The general laughter of the class suggests they have safely taken the comment as a joke.

"Wait till she starts dating and drinking and smoking," she would add. For Julie, all three were inseparable acts that occurred simultaneously as frequently as possible. The loud conversations no one else was supposed to hear suggested that most weekends and many weeknights were devoted to dating, drinking, and smoking.

"I'm pretty sure she won't ever leave the house when she's a teenager."

"Ha—you're gonna go nuts." Mercifully, this point of the conversation was usually when a classmate would point out that my girl was only two—that there were many years to go before that time.

I have to admit there were times when I was convinced I hated Julie more than I have ever hated anyone before. I hated that she was rude. I hated how easy it was for her to insult her classmates with her venomous (oftentimes literally infected) tongue. I hated that she saw me as insignificant, as evidenced by the way she would flaunt her disobedience daily. She ate chips and drank soda freely in the room. She sent and received text messages without any concern for the school-day ban on cell phones in the classroom. Her voice had only two volumes: loud and louder. The louder voice was usually reserved for saying something inappropriate and then scolding the class for listening in on her private conversations, such as when she asked another girl for a tampon so loudly that students outside in the hall could have heard her.

Even when trying to take her background into consideration, it was hard to separate her disease from who she was as a person. Her doctor wanted to experiment with her lithium dosage. Specifically, the doctor wanted to try taking her off it all together. The results were horrifying. When a bipolar 17-year-old girl with a total lack of self-control is on medication to try and rein in outrageous behavior, one can easily imagine the outcome. Even though she was only three feet away from me, she shouted that this was going to be a great weekend—a long Thanksgiving weekend—because she was going to stay sober.

"Good," I replied as nonjudgmentally as possible. I had been burned by Julie's overreactions in the past, so I had learned to try and direct all comments to her as blandly as possible to avoid seeming either overtly hostile or setting myself up to be the butt of her foul-mouthed humor.

"Why would you do that?" a friend asked.

"Because I drank way too much last weekend!" she laughed in response.

I tried to ignore her daily class proclamations that half the people in the school smoke and three fourths get drunk every weekend, just as most of her classmates ignored her, but one day when she said, "I guarantee you, half the girls in this school are sluts," I knew something had to be done. Since we were in journalism, I tried to redirect the class's attention—use what's referred to as a teachable moment.

"You know, Julie, you bring up a point I've been wanting to remind everyone about. You have a responsibility to write your articles with precision. You need to be careful about using words like *half* or *majority* if what you really mean is *many*."

She rolled her bulging bug eyes and sneered.

"I know this for a fact," she snorted. "I talk to people. I swear this is all true."

I had heard enough. "If you can point to a reputable study that has been conducted, or if you have firsthand knowledge of the private behavior of over one thousand of our students—an actual majority—then you can use words like *over half*. Until then, please just don't say anything at all."

I wanted to say, "Until then, shut your mouth you fucking bitch before my head explodes from pent-up rage," but teachers aren't supposed to say those things, so I ground my teeth and clenched my jaw.

Among all the websites providing free blog and networking space for anyone who wants to join, MySpace is the undisputed granddaddy of them all. All the kids talk about it. I had heard comments about it now and then without realizing just how huge it is. Hundreds of thousands of kids around the country bare their souls through the impersonal world of e-communities populated by e-friends. The national media finally started to pay attention to the power of MySpace because of a number of high-profile cases of violence stemming from acquaintances that started with innocuous online chatting, but it flew under most adults' radars for quite some time.

When Julie spent one class day checking messages people had posted on her site instead of her editorial assignment, I decided to see what she was up to. Our school has been exponentially expanding and improving its technology, and on this particular day our class had been using one of the mobile computer labs created a year ago. These carts are stocked with 15 laptops with wireless Internet and network access. I watched Julie carefully as she returned her laptop at the end of the hour. As soon as the students left, I began to view the history folder in her Web browser to see where she had been. I was fascinated and horrified to come across her MySpace profile and see that she was even more vulgar, more sexually explicit, and more forthcoming about her drug and alcohol adventures than in the classroom. She showed such little restraint in school that I couldn't imagine she could be much worse in private, but I was wrong. Maybe I was lacking in imagination, maybe it was just wishful thinking, but I thought I had seen and heard the worst of Julie. Her blog detailed regular drinking, regular drug use, the trauma of experiencing a miscarriage, and more profanity than I had seen in one place since reading a David Mamet play years ago.

Saying Julie had a short fuse would be an understatement, but her temper was worse than a lack of patience. If she ever felt wronged, she retaliated threefold. Another girl in the same journalism class supposedly called Julie a slut. Whether or not this really occurred was irrelevant. A friend of Julie's told her about it secondhand, so to Julie there was no doubt. The world of MySpace and similar blog sites has created a whole new problem for schools and students, in part because of the slippery nature of trying to address problems that take place outside the school's domain. Blogs and messaging have given rise to the alarming phenomenon of cyber-bullying. Julie posted several messages to the girl's MySpace page with comments like, "Sorry to hear about you caught S.T.D.s," and, "You're a skanky whore."

I printed off pages of Julie's blog and returned the laptop to the cart. That night I explored the pages in greater detail at home, where I discovered other disturbing declarations of destructive behavior—even a community ring known as "RHS Alcoholics." The next morning, Julie was the first to arrive in the room. "I'm having a bad day, Mr. Miller. Just so you know—in case I go off."

She made her best attempt at muttering under her breath, but her muttering was plainly audible to anyone entering the room. Discretion was not her strong suit. She buried her head in her arms on the desktop and fidgeted so violently I seriously wondered if she was hopped up on some kind of stimulant. "Fucking bitch. I'm going to go off . . ."

Leading her out to the hallway, I offered her two choices: go to the counselor to vent or go to the office and follow through on her empty threat to file harassment charges against the girl who allegedly commented on Julie's sexual behavior.

"I think I'll go to the office," she said, "because I want them to know my side of the story before something happens. She messed with the wrong bitch." It was survival mode for me. Every time she swore, every time she was excessively rude, every time her random outbursts made it clear she was either swallowing pills she shouldn't or not swallowing the ones she should, I tended to let it slide. When she was a freshman, I tried to control it. Now that she was a senior, I was trying to choose my battles more pragmatically. Or maybe it was just that I was afraid of her. I firmly believed in my gut that she was all talk, but I tasted vomit in my mouth whenever she looked at me with that ugly sneer, looked at my daughter's picture, and made some reference to when my "little girl grows up." She could find my house easily. She could find my daughter easily. It's not that I think she would commit any crime against me or my family, but I know she would delight in torturing me by showing up at the local playground and making me horribly uncomfortable. I suddenly wish I didn't live so close to my students. This student, at least. The way she projects all her problems onto the nearest authority figure means I am doomed to someday be the source of all her misery. I don't want to be this close when Julie tells me I've messed with the wrong bitch.

CHAPTER 14

Pinocchio Almost Killed Me

ANNE FRANK NEARLY KILLED ME. It's not her fault, really. Such an important figure in world history deserved nothing but the best, I thought. Pinocchio almost killed me too, but I guess that one was mostly my fault.

I was fairly inexperienced as a technical director when I arrived at my current teaching position and eagerly signed my contract to tech direct five productions. I had worked on my share of set construction crews, studied design, and worked most every aspect of theater. The quality and scale of the productions were what made the job appealing to me. I had very little interest in driving so far to show up in a small, almost rural town to work at a school no one ever heard anything about, but then I saw the theater; I saw the stage, scene shop, booth, and green room . . . all the spaces many schools—including some colleges—would envy. I came and saw a performance of *Godspell* that left me breathless, and I accepted the job offer. I wasn't going to be the head theater director, but working in such an exemplary program in any capacity was great consolation.

My previous experience in technical direction at the high school level consisted of small shows of my own design, working with a few kids and almost no budget. *Pinocchio* was the first play of the 1999–2000 season, my first play at the school, and my first experience being completely in charge of a student crew building someone else's design. The school had an ongoing working relationship with a technician from the Guthrie Theater, and he was the regular scenic designer for our shows. It didn't take long to discover the arrangement was going to be a painful one.

The kids weren't sure what to make of me, so they spent most of their time testing me. They wanted to know how hard I would push them to be productive, how many dirty jokes I would ignore, how reckless they could be with their safety. Meanwhile, I sat and tried to decipher design plans as they trickled in—tried to figure out how to take what I was seeing and turn it into instructions for kids to execute. The kids tried to figure out what in the world I was saying whenever I gave instructions.

A couple of particularly reckless ninth-grade boys, with no regard for safety or my growing frustration, decided to take charge of a project. One wall of Gepetto's shop was designed to sit in one position to serve as the exterior wall and then swing open like a page in a book to reveal an interior setting. Our initial attempt at constructing the wall to be as light as possible to ease the movement resulted in a wobbly wall that moved any way but easily. We were discussing the theory that making the wall thicker may help to stabilize it, and in a flash the boys began to disconnect parts and pieces. Before I knew what was happening, the entire structure was loosened to the point of complete instability and toppled over with one of the boys still in the middle of it.

The boy was fine, but at that point I realized I was in for something of a bumpy ride for the rest of the year. Even if the sets didn't fall apart, each show that year pushed me to my physical, intellectual, and emotional limits. The design for *The Diary of Anne Frank* re-created the secret attic apartment in a manner that combined elements of realistic reconstruction and stylistic expressionism. The sprawling set was probably as large as the actual apartment, if not larger. Massive beams suspended at awkward angles suggested being within the peak of the roof. Those massive beams worried me from construction to hanging through each and every performance. It wasn't until all the beams were resting on the ground being disassembled that I could breathe a sigh of relief.

The beams were only a piece of the larger puzzle that plagued me with that show. I spent night after night laboring over the seemingly endless cycle of scratching my head while looking at plans, building a section, discovering it didn't fit everything else, rebuilding it, cursing repeatedly, and then slapping myself all the way home to avoid dozing off. More than one night I drove home at 5:00 AM just to shower, change clothes, kiss my wife, and turn around to go back and teach. Not that I was of much use as a teacher those days.

Over time the learning curve kicked in, I became more efficient, and the frequency of graveyard shifts of set construction gradually declined. For the first four or five years, though, there were times when I was certain I was losing my mind. I suffered wild mood swings induced by serious sleep deprivation. I was useless at home and at work. I felt trapped financially, because neither teaching nor my extracurricular stipends could support my family alone, and yet doing both was eating me alive. It may have seemed reasonable at the time to bite the bullet, do what was best in everyone's interests, and cut back the workload. It always seemed we got by on whatever money we had, so we probably would have adjusted to a little bit smaller income. That may have been the reasonable thing to do, but my passion for that aspect of my career was anything but reasonable. I have always loved the creative energy of the theater. Even as I floundered those first years, every time a show was about to open I would take a moment to sit alone in the seats, oftentimes M19, and look at the stage. Obvious flaws in the set would nag at me and details we never completed made me wish for another week, but in the end I felt a certain sense of pride that I did that. Large or small, simple or complex, every set was a tangible accomplishment I could point to and say, "This is what I've been doing."

Maybe that's part of why I always ended a show feeling satisfied, even if the process made me want to drive off a bridge. Much of what I hate about teaching is that lack of concrete results. Since test scores and data are unimportant to me, all I have to hope for is that my students learn something, gain an appreciation for literature, and find their own voices to express themselves with a little sophistication in their written and spoken communication. I rarely see any sign that either of these things has taken place. I can't ask my family to come to my classroom, point to some students, and say, "Can you believe I made this?" Even if I could, which would likely creep the students out, I couldn't take credit for a student's education when it is so complexly comprised of years of encounters, thousands of lesson, and dozens of teachers. A set is something I brought into this world and eventually took back out.

I suppose it's for all of these reasons that I approach my work in the theater with greater passion and effort than my daytime teaching obligations. I tell my students to do the opposite. Make academics the priority, I tell them. Take care of your classes first before committing to the extracurricular work, and yet I am a walking poster child for extracurricular activities proving detrimental to classroom quality.

There are a number of teacher stereotypes out there, including the jock: The guy who probably teaches social studies, frequently talks about last night's big game as much as the class curriculum, and might even tell his classes to call him "Coach." I sometimes wonder if anybody realizes that there are non-jock versions of the coach in most high schools. I am about as nonathletic as they come, and yet if you replaced *game plan* with *set design*, and *last night's big game* with *this weekend's performances*, I'd be just as pathetically preoccupied as any coach in any high school.

I tell kids to make their classes the top priority, but I know they are just as likely as I am to let academics suffer in the spirit of "the show must go on." I hate what I put some of the most devoted kids through, but I'd be lost without them. I get dirty looks from fellow English teachers when they casually mention that Emily fell asleep in class and still hasn't turned in her essay on *The Great Gatsby*. Every year there are a handful of kids who are with me in the theater almost every minute that I'm there. If I hadn't wanted to cut back on the late nights for my family or myself, I'd surely feel the need to cut back for their benefit. They're driven, and I practically have to shake a two-by-four at them to get them to go home in the middle of the night when deadlines have passed and painting remains incomplete.

There must be some way to reconcile these conflicting emotions, but I'm still struggling to find it. I am, quite simply, unable to enjoy the aspect of my job that provides the most personal satisfaction because I end up overwhelmed with guilt for all the other aspects of my life and occupation that get less than they deserve. I know other people go through this; finding the precarious balance between work and home is a struggle millions have made before me, and millions more will take up the challenge every day that I teach. So what to do? Let me know if you figure it out. Right now I can't think about it anymore. I have a pile of essays on depictions of prejudice and courage in *To Kill a Mockingbird* under my desk waiting to be read and graded. I accidentally kicked the pile over, so I need to quickly straighten it up before I finish a sketch of my idea for a set and run down to the theater to adjust some lighting for next week's modern dance performance.

CHAPTER 15

Ode to Frivolity

M Y SISTER AND I HAVE A CAREFULLY REFINED RITUAL. She is a teacher too. Elementary music. Together, one humid August morning, we meet and mourn the summer that is about to slip away from us. We begin with coffee. Lots of strong coffee. Then coffee with Baileys Irish Cream. Then, when the mix of caffeine and alcohol begins to rot our empty stomachs, we order pizza and gorge ourselves. We spend the afternoon distended, taking in as much beer as possible whenever space frees up in our bellies. We laugh as much as we can, sometimes to the point of one or both of us snorting beer out our noses.

And we tell stories.

She tells me about a young boy in her school who frequently disappears for no apparent reason and can invariably be found in a hallway garbage can, his hiding place of choice. She tells me about a school secretary with a reputation for holding her liquor better than anyone, who places immigrant children into different grade levels with nothing more to guide her than the number of teeth in the child's mouth. About second-grade boys, seven years old, swearing at each other and barking out demands to their little girl classmates to suck their dicks in the middle of class.

I tell her about seniors who, because of idiocy or sloppiness, misspell simple words on major papers, sometimes even their own names. Students who admit suffering abuse but refuse to press charges, leaving us scratching our heads because if they're over 18 it's their call. I tell her about a morning when exhaustion had me by the throat, depression was sucking the drive right out of my body, and the kids just didn't give a shit. About how I curled up in a fetal position under my desk after they'd gone and cried. Lights off, door locked, and me under my desk as if I needed shelter from an explosion.

In August we can laugh at all of that. There may be only a handful of days left before the inevitable replay of a school year like any other school year, but at the moment we relish the company, the humor, the vulgarity. We feel sorry for ourselves, but at least we can walk into our staff workshops knowing that we had a day entirely devoted to drowning in alcohol every sorrow our jobs give us.

Once the school year begins and I find myself in need of cheering up, other diversions need to be found . . . and there are so many options when it comes to having fun at students' expense. Kids quickly discover that I'm not to be trusted, because trying to convince them of bald-faced lies is one of my favorite activities. Sometimes it works too well, and the lie comes back to haunt me. The first week of school I casually mentioned that another teacher in the room at the time had been an Olympic diver. I make up so much shit like that so rapidly that I assume none of it sticks, but six months later a ninth-grade boy asked that teacher why he never talks about his experience in the Olympics. I literally slapped my knees.

Whenever my classes ask me why I try to mess with their heads so much, I tell them, "Frustrating you—keeping you on your toes—golly, that's the best part of my job. I guess I have a sadistic streak." Okay, so in honesty it's probably not the *best* part of the job, but the kids don't need to know that. Not when they don't take anything I say seriously, anyhow.

However I do it, I relish being unpredictable. I want to be a unique experience in my students' school day. Maybe it is the innate entertainer in me, or it could be the power that comes from commanding their attention. I love to make them wonder about me. I might tell them a story about my childhood. Sometimes I tell them about my experience in elementary school learning to play the accordion at a studio that had accordion bands play every summer at a state hospital for mentally impaired adults. Playing the accordion was not necessarily the pathway to coolness in the first place, and I remember being fascinated and confused with the patients and their responses to a group of 20 little kids honking out semblances of familiar tunes. Some screamed, some clapped, others sat completely frozen except for the gradually growing glob of drool dangling from their open mouths.

Or I tell them about working my way through college as a campus security officer and getting called to deal with a "wild, naked man walking around campus." He was indeed wild, and he was indeed naked. He was tall and scrawny, leaping around the sidewalk on a frigid November morning. Technically off-duty when I was asked to respond by a deskbound coworker, I was not in uniform other than the utility belt and jacket. The wild man saw the patches and badge on the jacket and immediately turned his attention to me, showing off his karate moves and asking if I wanted to fight. He identified himself as an ex-Navy SEAL and explained that he was giving the university a peace demonstration before asking me if I want to fight again. I tell the classes about how I finally talked him into walking back to the security office with me to wait for the police and paramedics to arrive, but we had to pass several administrative offices along the way . . . all of which had glass doors . . . all of which had smudgy imprints of his body after we passed.

Just when they're about rolling on the floor at this guy's outrageous behavior, I tell them about meeting the man's mother the next night. About the heartbreak that emanated from her eyes as she told me about her son's mental illness and the wild episodes he experiences when he hasn't taken his medication. I lead them through the same roller coaster I experienced—laughing at that guy's expense one day, only to deeply regret it the next—wishing peace and calm for that man and his family. If they are really with me and unusually perceptive, they may even think twice about having laughed at my accordion story.

My side stories hopefully amuse the classes, but they have the potential to do even more than that. I approach my self-indulgent ramblings as diversions, but I am honest. I try to be a good storyteller, but I don't create stories. If kids really wanted to, they could figure out a lot about my psyche by examining the childhood experiences that made me who I am. One of the most telling glimpses into my composition comes when I tell them about my sister and the bedtime stories she often told me as a child. Inevitably they ask to hear one. Of course, I can't just tell them the story. I interrupt myself as frequently as possible with lengthy tangents to irritate them.

"My sister used to tell me stories about Sally and Sue," I tell them in a serious tone. I might pause for an uncomfortably long time, leaving the class to wonder if I'm going to say anything else.

"Sally and Sue were two young girls who often played together." I let the story trail off again, switching into commentary mode and saying, "You know, every now and then I thought they were real kids and I might bump into them in the vegetable aisle of the grocery store, but there wasn't much chance of that happening, because my aversion to vegetables made such an encounter unlikely."

If I'm lucky, that line gets a courtesy laugh. If I'm really lucky, everyone is too busy wondering what the hell is going on to fake a giggle.

"One fine day," I declare in a singsong voice, "Sally decided to go over to Sue's house to play. They weren't playing very long, though, before they began to fight. While they were fighting, Sue got mad at Sally and shoved her arm down the garbage disposal."

Nervous laughter or genuine laughter. Either way, I am pleased with myself.

"Sally didn't like losing her arm in the garbage disposal, and she was mad at Sue, so she went home. The next day, Sally forgot all about their fight and went back over to Sue's house to play. Sure enough, they got in another fight, and this time Sue shoved Sally's other arm down the garbage disposal. Sally went home armless and angry, but she wouldn't stay angry for long."

At this point I might stop for effect, possibly sipping coffee nonchalantly like George Burns chomping on a cigar before moving on with sudden enthusiasm.

"The next day, Sally walked back down the street to Sue's house, and, sure enough, they got into another fight. This time Sue shoved one of Sally's legs down the garbage disposal, so Sally left and hopped home.

"Keep in mind I was only seven at the time, so foolishly I didn't really know how utterly impossible all of this would be. I mean, really, what kid could hop all the way home on one foot?"

At this point, the class doesn't know anymore if any of this is true, in which case they're concerned, or they think it might be a really bad joke, in which case they're not impressed.

"The next day Sally hopped back to Sue's house. It didn't take long before another fight erupted and Sally rolled home legless. The next day her body was dispatched. The day after that, Sally rolled back to Sue's house for the last time. Sue and Sally's head got in one last fight, and Sue shoved Sally's head down the garbage disposal.

"The next day, Sally's mother noticed she was missing and went over to Sue's house to ask if anyone had seen her. Sue explained what had happened, and Sally's mother had the septic tank dug up so they could get Sally's pieces out and sew them back together. The next day, Sally went over to Sue's house to play."

Some sort of groan follows. Amusement, annoyance, maybe just a grunt because they couldn't figure out what other sound to make.

Then, as if nothing had happened, "So we were about to read about Odysseus's journey to the land of the Cyclops. Here we go." I drop the subject and move on without hesitation, because half of my amusement stems from the irony of devoting so much time to something I have no intention of discussing or even attempting to make relevant.

Lest I should become a bore when I run out of my own stories, I read Chuck Shepherd's syndicated column "News of the Weird" for my classes every Thursday. I cannot provide much of a rationale to defend devoting ten minutes of class once a week to sharing tidbits about the most unusual aspects of humanity, but I enjoy it. I enjoy it, and the kids enjoy it. They devour stories of incompetent criminals shooting themselves during attempted robberies, bizarre scientific studies documenting mating habits of giant jellyfish, and tales of people meeting their fates in terribly undignified ways using the famous last words of "Hey, look at me!" before losing their delicate balance on a balcony railing.

One thing I learned early on is how important the silly moments like this become for students. I could run into a student on the street years after he graduates, and all he'll be able to remember about his time in my class is that I read that "weird news thing." For a moment, it's flattering. For anything about my class to be remembered is impressive. For that memory to be a fond one is remarkable. And yet, whenever I encounter a comment like this one, I walk away feeling a little uncertain.

What kind of reputation am I earning? Is my ode to frivolity misguided? The tightrope walk between what is worthwhile for holding interest and what squanders valuable educational minutes is not a problem I have spent much time worrying about. Which is why I'm so perplexed to find myself disappointed when a former student says, "Still doing nothing in your classes? That was the best."

My playful side constantly seeks amusement for myself. My cynical side insists that anything that keeps the students—that toughest of crowds—under control is fair game. Combined, my senses of playfulness and cynicism tell me it's all okay. The kids tell me that playfulness is why I am so popular and everyone says I'm so cool. I tell them I've never been popular or cool. I try not to worry about what a couple of kids say to me years after memory has faded. It's the sad lot that most of the impact teachers have on their kids won't materialize until years later, and even then the kids might not be able to consciously trace their influences back to specific teachers. It's okay; I already knew all of this. Keep playing and we'll get by.

So why am I now wishing for more? What would it be like to be stopped on the street and thanked for breaking the code of Shakespearean language by a kid who used to think it was pure gibberish? For getting someone to see that literature is more layered than she thought, with depth limited only by her curiosity?

I know why I don't wish for more. Wishing for more leads to disappointment. Frivolity pays off.

I am an expert marksman with rubber bands. Armed with nothing more than a common variety pack of office-supply rubber bands, I can both entertain and discipline a class for weeks. I can snipe a sleeping boy in the back of the head from across the room without more than a second's hesitation in my oral reading. Students make targets on the backsides of their vocabulary quizzes, hold them up, and I oblige with a quick snap. The good rubber bands, the fat ones, sometimes even tear right through the page.

I know this is horribly irresponsible. I know the potential to hurt someone should be far more important to me than a desire to amuse the class and myself. Not to mention the influence I have on the kids—especially the boys—who instantly enter into a pissing match of sorts, trying to one-up me. It doesn't take long before rubber bands have gone astray and kids are diving for them on the floor.

One of these days someone will get seriously hurt. I already got lucky with one errant shot that came dangerously close to a boy's eye. A few millimeters more and there could have been a lawsuit pending. I made a point of checking on him and apologizing in front of the class. It was bad enough I had screwed up; I didn't want to make matters worse by acting as if I hadn't. He was okay, and I cut back on the rubber band shots. For a while. I berated myself for being careless, and then I berated myself some more when the temptation to try a trick shot now and then became too great.

Stop it! Who's the adult here?

Who *is* the adult here? Is it possible that years of surrounding myself with adolescents have made me less mature instead of me inspiring them to act more mature? I get great pleasure from all these silly things—the stories, the newspaper column, the rubber bands—but when should my obligation to be a professional override my simple pleasures?

Who knows, and who cares? Leave me alone. Close the door on your way out. There's an ugly blue patriotic stuffed bear hanging on the whiteboard. Someone left it in the room, and now it's calling my name. I'm going to brush aside the stack of essays that have been patiently waiting for weeks to be read, put my feet up on the desk, and shoot some rubber bands at that homely bear.

You won't tell on me, will you?

CHAPTER 16

Settling—Part II

S O, IF I REALLY HAVE MADE A HORRIBLE MISTAKE BY BECOM-
ING A TEACHER, as I frequently wonder, the question remains
of what else I should do. I have eight years of experience teaching
14- to 18-year-olds, a bachelor's degree in English and theater arts with
a minor in education, and not much else. None of my early jobs offered
anything resembling a career opportunity—working campus security
in college for a whopping seven dollars an hour, cashiering for a tiny
office-building convenience store, selling cameras, making pizzas . . .
the only job outside of education I have ever held that I could have
possibly parlayed into a career was my four month stint in the pets and
lawn and garden departments at Wal-Mart. I could have tried to work
my way up the corporate ladder of the universe Sam Walton built, but
something told me I wouldn't get anywhere with my shaggy hair and
noticeable lack of a southern drawl.

Still, on the really bad days I can't help but wonder what other
options may exist. I start exploring job listings to look for possibilities. I like to write, so maybe somebody would pay me to be a writer.
All of the writing positions I find are for technical writing or editing

copy before printing. Something about proofreading the latest annual report on the investment returns for chicken feed at the local poultry farm doesn't seem like a step in the right direction.

It would be really handy if a new career paid a lot more than teaching. That would be just swell, I think to myself, so I look for high-paying jobs. There are all sorts of them in management. I consider the qualifications and decide it could be argued that what I have done for ten years is basic management. I keep 30 or more young adults following a certain behavioral expectation on a regular basis. I try to balance my motivating praise with some motivating threats. I give grades and comments on report cards—a basic version of the periodic performance review. I could even argue that I manage budgets through my work with theater, including hiring assistants and dividing funds among project requirements. I think all of these things translate nicely, so clearly I ought to be hired to sit behind a desk in a corner office, earn six figures, and occasionally write reviews of how I believe my subordinates are doing.

Most businesses offering six-figure salaries for managers, though, seem to think teaching is not the exact equivalent to business management that I like to think it is. Besides, I hear those business types spend all their time dealing with numbers. I would rather find myself buried in a seemingly incomprehensible sea of words than an incomprehensible sea of numbers on profits, losses, revenues, expenses, assets, and liabilities.

There are other business jobs that might value my experience a little more, such as training, but then I'm facing a job that won't pay any more than teaching, won't allow as many days off as teaching, and will require more expensive and uncomfortable attire than teaching.

Maybe I could get a job as a theater director. After all, the work I do with plays is some of the most gratifying time spent on the job. I would love to take my craft to the next level, apply all I have learned through work on dozens of plays, and express my creativity on a full-time basis. I suspect, though, that professional theaters, much like businesses, would scoff at my experience as beneath them. It's as if the whole world subscribes to the notion that people who teach do so because they weren't good enough to pursue their subject professionally. Not to mention I would have no job security working from production to production, as well as no benefits—no health insurance or retirement . . . all those necessities of life for an adult with a family needing to live responsibly.

What else would I do . . . Depending on just how bad the day was that spurred such daydreaming, the realization that there is no better fit anywhere can either be reaffirming or depressing. I could end my job search relieved as I remember how rare it is for a job to encompass everything I like most about teaching, or I might log off the job-listing sites feeling utter despair at the notion of never finding a job that truly suits me.

I convince myself I am a malcontent and that I constantly dwell on anything I don't like to the exclusion of anything I do. I know I am wasting my time whenever I daydream of some perfect, high-paying job that doesn't exist. And I know that it's not because I am a malcontent. It's not just me; everywhere around me people wonder if this is as good as it gets, but that doesn't stop me from wondering.

CHAPTER 17

Student Profiling

FOR BETTER OR WORSE, humans tend to have an innate desire to categorize the world around them. When we see something or someone, we try to figure out how this new person or thing compares and fits in with all else that we know. The educational system is full of all sorts of categories, some formal (honors kids, athletes, free-lunch program kids, etc.) and some informal cliques (skaters, Goths, jocks, etc.). I oftentimes find the labels to be lacking. What follows are the categories that really provide the best representation of the modern student body.

My portraits are broken down by gender, because in this hotbed of hormones and pubescence the difference between boys and girls is as stark as it'll ever be. First, the boys:

A-ADHD

Recent accounts and studies suggest that attention-deficit/hyperactivity disorder may be overdiagnosed in cases in which boys are simply active individuals, but I firmly believe that there are cases where a disorder exists. My first personality profile is aggressive ADHD. It may seem redundant to label a boy with ADHD as aggressive, but this is a particular species. Distinguishing features include a propensity for hat stealing and a penchant for random punches to the arms. The boy may be on the football or hockey team, but he will most likely quit before reaching any noticeable degree of success because of the increased demands for discipline, focus, and effort as he approaches the varsity-level years.

Social Comedian

Sometimes also referred to as the class clown, but there's much more to it than clowning around. This is not a matter of performing antics out of a simple desire for attention and approval. These boys have adeptly integrated humor into their repertoire of coping skills—and they have plenty of need for coping skills—because they are almost invariably at one physical extreme or another. The puny, prepubescent boys are the most vocal and active comedians, while the particularly obese boys tend to have a quieter, wittier sense of humor. They are likely to mutter intelligently sharp insults under their breath and recite lines from Monty Python without notice from their classmates.

Quiet, but Adjusted

These boys are friendly and pleasant. Their academic intelligence runs the gamut, but the smarts that matter seem to be developing just fine. That is, they know the importance of treating others well, which will take them far in their future lives as husbands, fathers, employees, and citizens. For now, though, they are painfully introverted. Introversion is not without its benefits. These sensitive boys who talk less tend to become better listeners. These are the students I frequently see smiling and laughing silently when I make an inappropriate joke just quietly enough that anyone talking or not paying attention would never know they missed it.

Quiet, but Maladjusted

Very little scares me more than these boys. They are an absolute mystery, silently drifting through the educational system, waiting for the day they graduate with no fanfare. They lack motivation, and yet they keep showing up. Sure, attendance is mandatory, but that doesn't stop many of these boys' counterparts from skipping. The boys who are obviously stoned don't scare me so much, but the ones who are lucid yet still display no personality or human interaction skills are ticking time bombs.

These are the quiet kids next door that the neighbor on the evening news talks about after the family is found chopped to death with an ax, saying such familiar lines as, "He never bothered no one. He was quiet, pretty much kept to himself. Never woulda known he was gonna do somethin' like this." The range of possible descriptors is wide. Some like to single out Goths or skaters. Others point to the bullying victim with an unfortunate case of hideous acne. The only sure way to identify a boy of this category, as unscientific as the method may be, is to look in his eyes. There's something in the eyes: an unsettling combination of defiance and despair. The defiance and despair silently feed off each other, creating an unstable chemical reaction that either rots out the core of the lost boy or erupts in a violent explosion. In either case, the kid who quietly went unnoticed day in and day out meets with an unhappy ending. Sometimes dead, sometimes living dead, but never as a living, breathing, fully functional human.

These are the boys everyone started trying to profile post-Columbine. The problem, though, is that this group cannot be pinned down any more specifically than what I have done here. Experts may have developed more concrete indicators and such, but overall these kids are disturbingly hard to read.

And now for the girls . . .

Jock Girls

These fairly well-liked girls are driven to succeed. Note that basketball players are not included in this category, because boys already feel threatened enough by athletic girls as it is, and so being athletic and tall tends to dampen the basketball girl's chance at widespread popularity. The ones who thrive in this category are physically fit from frequent activity, a trait that certainly can't hurt in the image-driven high school. Soccer players and volleyball players do the best, with runners not too far behind. In terms of academic ability, girls generally do better than boys, though that's sometimes more a matter of work ethic than true ability. Jock girls who already push themselves in their sport usually maintain good academic discipline as well.

The Beautiful Witches

This is the thankfully small group of girls responsible for a series of fashion trends that bring heart attacks to fathers everywhere. Just when it seemed that it couldn't get any worse than spaghetti-strapped tanks with exposed bra straps, along came what had to be the most uncomfortable fad ever: the thong worn under low-rise jeans. These same girls are unnaturally tan, blonde, and skinny. They may make an attempt at athleticism, but rarely get beyond the dance team. The insecurity that fuels their constant need to beautify themselves is only made worse by the accompanying air of superiority they attempt to project. Most likely student to apply makeup in class; also most likely to roll eyes when asked to stop.

The Artists

Closet poets dreaming of winning magazine teen poetry contests, skilled artists with a knack for sketching friends and horses, dancers who shun the kick line to study modern dance, singers who don't try to sound like a pop star. These girls find satisfaction through self-expression. They provide the balance in a culture that worships prescribed looks, popularity, and sports. Ranging wildly from the mute with hair blocking the outside world from seeing her face to a gifted artist who can actually claim without exaggeration to be everyone's friend. Regardless of temperament or social prominence, these girls give the school soul.

The Homebodies

Unfortunately, there are some girls who don't excel at sports, don't have the looks the beautiful witches possess, and lack the success the artists have found. That's not to say they haven't tried to be any of those things, but when met with failure they succumb rather than persevere. They may be avid readers. They are likely to provide a substantial amount of care for much younger siblings at home. Their handwriting is good but their grammar is not. Unlike the maladjusted boys, these girls are not likely to explode when everything falls apart. Instead, they wither. At the most they implode.

Such profiling is probably worthless. Sometimes, though, generalizations contain kernels of truth. These generalizations contain my kernels of truth as I have perceived them from my vantage point. There are always going to be exceptions and individuals can cross over to multiple types, but these descriptions accurately describe the vast majority of my students: our children.

If perpetuating stereotypes pisses people off, good. Prove me wrong. It is not my intention to belittle or demean my students, but ask any teacher who has been at it for awhile and they will tell you that patterns emerge. Some similarities are just too profound to be ignored.

I frequently run into the professionally awkward situation of students wanting to tell me about other teachers and their classes. Specifically, they want to rant and complain. Sometimes it's a conversation held in my presence that makes me uncomfortable even if I'm not directly involved (I don't need my colleagues thinking I'm a gossip with my students). Other times kids seek out my thoughts on encounters they've had with teachers. Really they're hoping a teacher will validate their complaints and bolster their sense of superiority over the problematic teacher in question.

Since no good can come from engaging in these kinds of conversations, I do my best to remain uninvolved. When kids do draw me in, I always try to hypothetically offer a perspective that could explain or rationalize a colleague's actions without really knowing the whole story. Usually I can get a kid to realize he may have contributed more to whatever conflict unfolded than he originally was willing to admit. Sometimes I think the stories can't possibly be true, only to find out otherwise from another teacher. Most of all, the stories offer some glimpses into other classrooms, like a peek in the unsuspecting host's medicine cabinet, which paint a pretty strong painting. Maybe not an entirely accurate one, but vivid all the same.

Just as I do my best to avoid engaging in teacher trash-talking with my students, I am trying to keep this book about my own strengths and weaknesses without passing judgment on others. Through my own years as a student, however, up through my current point in my educational career, I have come up with a few categories for my fellow high school teachers as well. It's only fair, I suppose, to shine the spotlight back on us after dissecting the student body. In no particular order, these are some common species of high school teachers:

Newspaper Readers

Neither time of year nor time of day seems to matter to these teachers. Stumble upon them and invariably it seems all they have to do is blankly scan the pages of newspaper sprawled out before them. No other pressing tasks. No assignments to grade, no plans to make, just sit and read the paper. Oftentimes teachers with a great deal of seniority, their lessons seem to have been refined over the course of years to a set routine that can be recited by rote without any need or desire to modify based on changing times or student needs. That must be a relaxing, horribly unexciting world to inhabit.

Martyrs

Clearly martyrs exist in careers other than education, but the teaching martyr is a prevalent breed. It also comes in two distinct varieties: the actual humble martyr and the martyr by design. The actual humble martyr is a teacher who quietly puts in twice the contracted work hours, shows up early and leaves late, all in the name of preparing to be the best teacher possible. He or she might spend hours on providing exhaustive feedback on assignments. The self-discipline these teachers possess, and their willingness to give so much of themselves to their classes, has always impressed me. I have even come across one or two who make me want to be a better teacher, such as the colleague in my department I felt compelled to nominate for Minnesota Teacher of the Year. When several students and I completed the nomination, she thanked us sincerely for the thoughtfulness of the nomination but stated she would not pursue the award. She wasn't in it for recognition.

The martyr by design, contrarily, thrives on ensuring everyone within earshot knows just how hard he or she works. Constant complaints about too much to do without enough time litter even the briefest comments while passing in the hall. This species is prone to sighs and offering unsolicited updates about how little sleep was had the previous night. It seems likely that everyone has encountered this type somewhere. Their most infuriating trait is the unstated suggestion, with each reminder of just how hard they're working, that no one else could possibly have just as much going on.

I readily admit I've been the martyr by design on more than one occasion, though I never consciously tried to suggest others had it any easier. I simply needed a little sympathy before bucking up and heading back into battle.

Curmudgeons

They should have retired 20 years ago. Kids are the enemy, every new policy initiative is a farce, and they are counting days to retirement—even though it's still six or seven years away. For all practical intents and purposes, though, they've already mentally retired. Kids will wait out the countdown with these teachers, stuck in a preretirement purgatory they can do nothing about. Sometimes the curmudgeons become quite popular teachers. This occurs when the checked-out teacher gives up completely, no longer bothering with lessons, assignments, or tests, and instead relying on telling stories about the days of yore or ranting about the current event of the teacher's choice. The curmudgeons who stick to their guns, though, and work under the mentality that their students should listen because they said so find themselves in endless power struggles. May or may not double as a newspaper reader.

Cheerleaders

These Pollyannas are annoying either by sincere positivism or by phony, nauseating ass-kissing. Every new idea put forth by administration is brilliant, every trivial accomplishment by students or staff is cause for applause, and every time I see them in action I double my efforts to be a sarcastic cynic.

Newbies

It's always fascinating to watch someone start a teaching career. Student teaching is a fair introduction to the demands of the job, but by its very nature the entire experience is the equivalent of riding a bike with training wheels for four months, only to have the wheels taken off at the top of a steep hill—and no helmet and no brakes. Many could do just fine with such an experience after four months tooling around with their training wheels, but plenty of others wipe out. A number of states and districts are beginning to recognize the importance of various mentor programs so that these newbies in jeopardy of tumbling downhill can grab on for help now and then.

College professors tell their teachers-to-be that confidence is vital—kids will sense weakness and exploit it. To a certain extent this is true, but what gets left out of these overly simplistic lessons is that such confidence does not necessarily need to extend to staff meetings. At times a newbie who purports to have all the answers—they memorized them as their professors spoke them—can be amusing. Ah, naiveté. When that unjustified confidence continues and even dares contradict people who know of what they speak, well . . . then we just wish they would shut up.

CHAPTER 18

Open Letter Number 4

D EAR PARENTS,

Are you starting to get a little worried about leaving me alone with your sons and daughters? I assure you, I'm harmless. At worst I'll waste some time, fail to provide as thorough feedback on their essays as some of my martyr colleagues will. You *should* be worried, though. Your kids are tormented. Your school leaders are genuinely concerned about your kids, but all of their time is consumed managing budgets and sweating over your perceptions of the school. They worry about test scores. Oh so many test scores. And it's not as simple as high passing rates or having most kids performing proficiently. It's about being advanced. Being among the best. Whatever the state average, principals want their schools to be above it.

If you think I'm burned out, you should see some of the older teachers. One old woman who teaches math compulsively hovers over her papers. She scrutinizes every detail of every quiz, test, and worksheet. She hounds her students, calls them stupid (without even pretending to be joking, like me), and asks them (rhetorically, I assume), "What the fuck am I doing here?" if nobody can answer her questions. There are plenty of others like her. They're the ones you have to worry about. Me? I'll keep on trying to do my best when I feel like it and hope not to cause too much harm when I don't feel like trying.

I'll never admit this much to you in person, though. As much as my casual, disheveled appearance will allow it, I'll maintain an air of professionalism. I'll be calm and reassuring. I will even go so far as to sugarcoat the problems to avoid conflict and make you feel better about your kid. For example, parent-teacher conferences are a marathon exercise in maintaining false pleasantries and appearances. Allow me to walk you through the kind of conversation I have had literally hundreds of times, perhaps even with you. Only this time, let's dig beneath the surface. During plays, I will frequently conduct alternate versions of the dialogue taking place onstage with the techies backstage on headset. These alternate lines expose the blunt subtext. The following generic conference conversation has been translated into backstage subtext.

Parent: Hi—nice to see you again.

Parent: Oh, it's this guy. I remember him from the open house. He's the weird one that mumbles and cracks lame jokes.

Teacher: Good evening. Good to see you too.

Teacher: Again? Good to see you again? Should I remember you? Say your name. I don't know you by face—I may not even know your kid by his . . . her? . . . his face yet. I'm not standing up. Please don't think me rude. I won't even offer my hand to shake yours. My supervisor

*when I student taught made me paranoid about the colossal expo-
sure to germs of all kinds by shaking everyone's hands at conferences.
Oops, you were saying something and I wasn't listening.*

Parent: You have my daughter in English . . . (fumbling through
papers) sixth hour. She's Jessie.

Parent: All right. Whatever he says, don't show a reaction. Just listen.

Teacher: Oh, sure. Jessie's a great kid. Did you get a chance to see
her midterm progress report?

*Teacher: Which girl are you talking about? I have a Jess, Jessie, and a
Jessica. I suddenly can't remember which is which. Maybe if you have
the midterm with you, I'll see the last name and hopefully remember.*

Parent: No, she must not have brought it home.

*Parent: This is the third teacher to ask us about midterms. How dare
she hide them from us! How embarrassing.*

Teacher: That's okay. We can look at my printout.

*Teacher: All right, I figured out which one is in sixth hour. We're all set
to go. Oh, shit. This girl drives me nuts. Her voice grates on my nerves.
Her constant putzing with makeup. Her high-pitched cackle. She . . .*

Parent: How does it look?

Parent: Please let it be passing. I don't need an A. Anything but an F.

Teacher: Well, things seem to be okay.

*Teacher: I don't think she's failing. Depends on if she ever did the
essay from last month I still haven't looked through yet.*

Parent: And in class? How is she?

Parent: *Watch it, mister. I hear about what goes on in your class. Sounds to me like it's out of control. Single out my daughter and I'll haul you to the mat.*

Teacher: Well, you know, she's sociable and a bit more into her friends than class, but that's not terribly unusual for her age.

Teacher: *Chickenshit. Quit sugarcoating it.*

Parent: So, no concerns then?

Parent: *I don't believe you, but thank you for humoring me.*

Teacher: No. Just keep at it. I think she's capable of even more than she's doing now if she really applies herself, but she's doing fine as it is.

Teacher: *How's that for noncommittal? Who amongst us is not capable of doing more if we applied ourselves? God, I'm so full of it.*

CHAPTER 19

Companionship and Where It Got Us

Teaching is a lonely line of work. I find myself conversing via email during the course of the day with teachers next door to my classroom. The old-timers claim the worst thing that ever happened to faculty collegiality was the loss of the smoking lounges. While I certainly don't think a reduction in smoking is any great loss, I can see their point. It's astounding how much even an introvert like me begins to crave adult interaction. In that respect I have been fortunate. Not just fortunate—I've had a great scam running for years.

I have happily taken on ninth-grade English classes with a high concentration of special-education kids: students with an Individual Education Plan (IEP), providing them federally mandated protections and accommodations. Some of my colleagues automatically assume that special education means more work. True, there are oftentimes more details to remember and more flexibility demanded. And yes, sometimes the fears of wild, uncontrollable behavior prove true, but not nearly as often as some would suggest.

"You have all those special-ed kids?" someone might ask before adding, "I'm so sorry. You must have your work cut out for you."

"It's not so bad," I'll reply.

"Really? I don't know how you do it."

"It's actually not that much more work. I often find kids with learning disabilities are better in the classroom."

"You're just saying that."

"No, really. If a kid has to work harder to understand what he's reading, he often develops better work habits in general. If things don't come to them easily, these kids appreciate it more. They're actually more likely to enjoy learning for learning's sake than non-special-ed kids."

"Huh." The person, whoever it is, reacts almost as if she's disappointed. Maybe she doesn't like having her assumptions shaken up. Maybe she feels like I'm trying to sound superior in my handling of exceptional situations when others have struggled. This would be a mistake, because I can point to more examples of failure than would fit in this book.

In a required course like English, enough special-ed kids in one room can lead to calling in the reinforcements. If the theater program is the saving grace of my job, my English 9 classes are a close second. Not because the students themselves are that unique from any others, but because they are co-taught. Co-taught. What a wonderful thing.

Enough of the kids in my classes have *co-taught English* written into their IEPs that I get to work collaboratively with another teacher, one from the special-education department, in a sharing of classroom responsibilities. As long as I have been at my school, I have been assigned to co-teach with the same guy.

I had no idea what to expect when I first met Jason. All I had heard was that he was fresh out of college and was actually an elementary school teacher by training. I had only been teaching for one year myself, so I was a little concerned about the two of us inexperienced guys trying to get anything right. I didn't even know what co-teachers were supposed to do.

Jason was the kind of guy I probably wouldn't have known in high school. He was a football player through and through with a solid build, a competitive edge, and an aura of popularity. In the years I have since come to know him, it seems he's still in contact with dozens of close friends from a decade ago long after I've lost touch with virtually everyone I knew. In high school, differences such as those between Jason and me tend to make a big difference, but outside that social structure, commonalities are much more easily spotted.

We shared a fondness for *The Simpsons*, a passion for good beer, and a wickedly sarcastic sense of humor. Turned out that Jason too found a great deal of pleasure in lying to kids for the sake of messing with their heads. It was Jason who was passed off with surprising success as a former Olympic diver.

I wish every teacher could experience what we have: sharing classes with a close, personal friend. The restorative power of adult companionship cannot be overstated when one faces day after day of taxing adolescent immaturity. So what if we're just as likely as any of the kids to tell a bad joke, shoot a rubber band, or whine that we simply don't feel like working today? We are above the petty squabbles and woes of teen life, but it's far more satisfying to feel superior with a colleague around. What good is a feeling of superiority when there's no one to really share it with?

For the first few years we taught together, Jason was a stabilizing force. When I tried for the eighth time to answer a student's question about the Friar's scheme in *Romeo and Juliet* only to have my words drowned out by incessant chattering, Jason could step in. While I shook my head in frustration, he could use his broad-shouldered stature, deep voice, and sigh of exasperation to regain control. His training with elementary kids served him well in these times. Fourteen-year-olds can be remarkably like eight-year-olds.

A few years ago I reached a psychological low. These were the days when I felt like curling up in a ball under my desk and, once or twice, actually did. That was when I dreamed of a job in a cubicle writing some company's internal newsletter. I drank a little and wished I was drinking a lot. I recognized the same anxiety and despair that haunted me off and on throughout junior high, high school, and college. I was drowning. Kim was worried, I was worried, and our first child was on her way. I decided to get my ducks in a row and get the help I needed for everyone's sake. For my family, my students, and me.

Just as I was making my way out of an abyss of gloom for the third time in my life, life took Jason for a ride. He and his wife hadn't been married much more than a year when a traumatic crime drove them from the home that they had already worked so hard to make their own. Forced to move years before they expected to, Jason faced more stress courtesy of the state of Minnesota. Every year he lived the nightmare of the untenured teacher: laid off, hopeful but anxious, rehired, run through the gauntlet for another year, laid off . . .

A licensed teacher in Minnesota, in theory, ought to be safe with a room of kids regardless of their age. Of course, it's nice if that teacher is able to do some actual teaching, so there are some limits to how much a person can do beyond the scope of one's license. For example, Jason could teach high school special education because he had a license in *something*, because the school needed *somebody*, and because the school couldn't find *anyone*. And so he got a variance. As time went on and this new specialty seemed like a good fit, Jason began graduate school to get his license in special education. He invested thousands; all he wanted in return was to keep his job.

I firmly believe in the value of learning about teaching. I do not subscribe to the notion that "community experts" can become insta-teachers through some kind of crash course. However, I also believe that teachers aren't worth much their first few years, even if they studied teaching for years in college. It's all about the on-the-job training. In Jason's case, he was worth his weight in gold as a special-ed teacher with a successful track record and five years of experience. Yet the summer after his fifth year he was faced with the prospect of losing it all if he didn't get the official license. That summer he student taught. Again. Lucky bastard got to spend his recharge time—his grounding time—paying for the privilege to work without pay.

Then, when patience and savings were stretched thin, a botched auto-repair job led Jason to stop payment on the check to the incompetent mechanic. The mechanic, in turn, sued Jason for a payment past due. Just as I was starting to actually feel like I could do this job, life's obstacle course took Jason for a jarring ride. It almost seemed as if we couldn't both be happy at the same time. The burnout point I had reached just a few years ago was eating Jason, and for the first time I saw how painful it is to witness. He started saying some of the same things I used to say, cursing the kids and wondering how much longer a person could do this damn job.

Several years ago a local reporter did some substitute teaching and turned the experience into a feature story. The ending conclusion was sheer brilliance, and yet it did little to provide any relief or guidance. It said something along the line of, "Teaching is too hard on those who care and too important to be left to those who don't care." Our building is full of examples of this theory in practice: teachers beating themselves up by caring too much and others who disengaged years ago and are coasting through to retirement with blinders on.

Jason isn't the only one. There are a number of other teachers who are reaching their limits, and when I end up at the receiving end of their venting I find myself in the unfamiliar position of trying to offer encouragement. Most times people simply need to express their frustration to someone else who understands, so I don't make the mistake of trying to solve anyone's problems unless advice is explicitly requested. Instead, what teachers most frequently need is a chance to verbalize what's eating them, find some comfort in knowing others understand, and then laugh the anemic laugh of someone doomed to repeat the cycle over and over, fully aware of how absurd it all is.

After we'd been working together for a couple of years, Jason and I got a catalog in the mail for overseas tours geared toward high school students. The big exclamation on the front cover could not be missed: *First-time group leaders travel free with five paid students!* Wheels instantly began turning. We would both love to travel, and we would definitely love to travel for free. Other teachers took trips with their students. The foreign language teachers all occasionally organized trips to their respective countries, and a humanities teacher in the building had a long-standing tradition of leading a group of 30-plus kids on a 30-day, whirlwind tour of the European continent every other year. Choir group sometimes did the same, and the marching band found ways to travel to destinations as varied as Orlando, Europe, and China. The evidence that such a trip could work was all around us. Our spouses needed a little more convincing, and then there was the issue of whether we were surrounded by too many examples of successful trips. We were dealing with a finite pool of students with the interest and the means to travel abroad. Too much competition did not bode well for our master plan.

The first step, in our minds, was to find a niche that wasn't being filled. We weren't going to compete with any of the foreign language classes, and there were only so many kids to go on a major multicountry tour, so we decided to focus on our own experience teaching English together and, in my case, theater. It didn't take long to figure out London was calling, and we hoped the kids heard it too. The land of Shakespeare, paired with a few West End shows, seemed just the ticket for offering an experience to students that wasn't currently being offered. Jason and I had already taught *Romeo and Juliet* together so many times that people were open to the idea of us taking kids to see the rebuilt Globe Theatre.

We tentatively put out feelers in all directions. Would any students even want to go? Would any of them have the money? Would any parents trust their kids with a couple of young teachers traipsing around a different continent? Turns out, plenty of kids thought running around London with a couple of teachers sounded like a great time, and a few of their parents found it a good idea too. Well, they might not necessarily have thought it a good idea, but kids can be very persuasive when they decide they really want something. A handful of parents relented, and plans for the trip began to form in earnest.

Four months after we were committed to leading the tour, with over a dozen students committed to going with us, we watched the news in a shocked stupor as the events of 9/11 unfolded before our eyes. In the days that followed, questions began to arise about whether or not the trip would be canceled, whether individuals could cancel, and what all of this meant for families who had been investing precious cash on a trip for their children that they probably wished they could be taking themselves. If Jason and I were nervous about taking kids overseas on our own before, the stakes suddenly got a lot higher.

I still don't know if I would have flown if our tour had been scheduled much earlier, but since we didn't actually depart until the following July, ample time had passed to convince everyone that flying could be safe again. I say *could be* because, while everyone was outwardly confident, the possibilities and memories still swirled in our heads. Kim and I flew to take a vacation with her parents in December, and the lack of incident on that trip boosted my comfort level in July. The best thing I could do to ease the nerves of young travelers and their families was to exude confidence myself, and it was substantially easier to do having experienced the increased security screening and anxiety of flying in the post-9/11 months already.

We couldn't have been happier about our group. Jason, his wife Kelly, Kim, and I made up a young crew of group leaders. We had a comfort level with one another that allowed us to see the trip as a vacation for the four of us as much as a field trip for the kids. Of the kids, the first to sign up were from the core of devoted techies. Several guys who'd already spent more hours with me throughout the school year than with their own families were now about to spend nine days of their summer with me as well. The rest of our tour group was rounded out by kids who bought into our pitch. Some were interested in theater as casual actors/performers; some were interested in London and England as a whole because of the historical aspects: the land of Stonehenge and King Arthur myths and Jack the Ripper. There were 20 of us in all, and none of us had traveled abroad before.

One instant observation: kids are much more tolerant of inconveniences than adults. We stepped off the plane at Gatwick International exhausted from a nine-hour overnight flight where no one slept, everyone was stiff and sore, and all were in great need of a shower and a nap. We were anxious for a little adjustment time at the hotel, but what we got was a little bewilderment in the purgatory of the airport. Our guide was nowhere to be seen. Our instructions were to walk out of the international arrival area, walk up to the person holding the tour company sign, step onto our private coach, and enjoy the scenic drive into town. Jason and I cursed the missing guide under our breath while kids patiently sat with their luggage. We cursed the unfamiliar dialing system of England's telephones as we tried to contact our hotel for answers while kids smiled at each other, despite their bleary-eyed state, because they couldn't be happier to finally be in England after over a year of anticipation. Turns out a car accident had somehow ground the train system to a halt, where an equally frustrated guide sat helplessly as we sat in the airport. As we sat in the airport, a coach driver sat in the parking lot twiddling his thumbs. Our guide finally arrived, disarmingly charming and apologetic, and provided the missing link between passengers and transportation. Not a single kid complained during the entire delay.

The entire trip to the hotel was filled with pointing out this and that—look at the thatched roof over there, all the MINI Coopers and other tiny cars over there, the skyline of London coming up as we approached the Thames. The hotel itself was in an historic building with an impressive white stone facade. Identical buildings lined both sides of the street. The series of separate entrances made it impossible to tell how much of the building was the hotel or which doors led to private residences. As happy as we were to be at the hotel, we were told upon arrival that our rooms wouldn't be ready for several hours. The itinerary for the day called for an immediate walking tour to familiarize everyone with the area, to explain how to navigate traveling by tube, and (most importantly) to keep us moving so we were forced to remain active during the time we wished we could crash. The pain was for our own good, because the alternative meant taking days to adjust to the new time zone. Not a single kid complained.

And when we finally got into our rooms and discovered all the jokes about broom-closet-sized hotel rooms in Europe were true, we adults expressed dismay, but the kids all shrugged and found it rather amusing.

The 16 students were a delight. Jason and I readily admit we began planning the trip with selfish motivations, hoping to take the vacation of our dreams for free because a bunch of kids came along and paid their way. To us and to our wives, it was as if the students were an inconvenience that could be tolerated because of the larger benefit they provided. Of course, none of us was a parent yet. Bearing total responsibility for this crew for nine days created unexpected parental instincts, and we soon realized the joys of witnessing children discover the world.

We found the dome in St. Paul's Cathedral impressive, a quiet boy named Matthew found it awe-inspiring, and wished we had time in the schedule to climb the stairs to test the famed acoustics. We enjoyed browsing the four-story Doc Martens store at Covent Garden; Erik and Adam bought green and red plaid shoes and proudly wore them the rest of the week despite the blisters they earned breaking them in during days of intensive walking. We adults were a little disappointed in the blasé performance of *Fame*; the kids picked it apart with precise, sophisticated criticisms fit to make their theater teacher proud.

Don't get me wrong; it would be misleading of me to suggest those nine days magically became all about the kids and only the kids.

I place just as much value on the time Kim and I spent with Jason and Kelly in the many pubs of Britain—pubs that seemed too good to be true. Dark woodwork, brass rails, weathered hardwood floors, and draught beer like nowhere else I have ever been. The warm atmosphere, the instant familiarity of it all . . . each historic pub was a seductive siren luring me in for a pint. Perhaps it's for the best that I haven't felt the same thing anywhere else, because I could see myself wasting my life away in a pub if it were readily available. The sweet drowning in its own deliciousness. Probably best saved for the rare trip to London.

Despite the flawed service of the tour company, a record-setting week of extreme heat and humidity, and being paired with an obnoxious group of early-teen Girl Scouts and their equally loud and obnoxious mothers, the trip surpassed all our hopes. The kids were, in a word, inspiring. Listening to a bunch of teenagers talk about their favorite moments, one might expect to hear about horseplay late at night in hotel rooms or some other trivial incident. Matthew relished taking in *My Fair Lady* at the Drury Lane Theatre. Two quiet girls were taken with the beautiful town of Bath in the southwest corner of the country, home to both an exquisite cathedral and the ingenious hot baths left over from the halcyon days of the Roman Empire. Erik and Adam browsed used bookstores and urban punk shops like seasoned college intellectuals. Greg could have spent the entire week studying the historical collection of arms housed at the Tower of London. Everyone, myself included, was stunned by the awe-inspiring weight of history we found around every corner, in cobblestone alleys, and in the shadow of Big Ben.

During the sentimental chats in college classes about the nobility of the teaching profession, I imagined there would be some indescribable moments of transcendence, when I felt the stars were aligning, I was in full stride, and all was right in the world of education—including my rightful place in it. I hadn't felt it yet, not like I imagined it while daydreaming in those tedious lectures, after three years of teaching. I felt it those nine days in London.

In keeping with every other experience at my school, no success would go unpunished. Jason and I got along famously. We co-taught one to three classes for eight years, half of which had us based in the same classroom. We became virtually interchangeable. We could finish each other's sentences, read the other's thoughts with little more than a quick glance, and recognize points of concern among our students with clear precision. Our students expressed their delight each year at having us both in the room.

Jason helped students receiving services from special education feel like they were in the same boat as everyone else. One of our proudest moments came at the end of a school year. A student who had clearly forgotten our explanation at the beginning of the year asked about the teaching arrangement, as if suddenly realizing that he didn't have two teachers in all his classes. We explained that Jason was a teacher from the special-ed department, assigned to the class to help me deliver the content in the best way possible with a particular emphasis on meeting the needs of kids with an IEP.

"There's special-ed kids in here?" the boy asked, a look of genuine surprise on his face.

"Yes, there are," I replied.

"Who?" he wanted to know.

"That's not important . . ." Jason started to say in an effort to preserve confidentiality and avoid making any students uncomfortable.

"I am," one boy uttered as he raised his hand. He looked to Jason, then to me, as if to say *I am not ashamed.* Several other students in class raised their hands voluntarily, happy to claim their learning disabilities or emotional/behavioral disorders without fear of stigma or humiliation.

"All right then. That's cool," the boy responded, content that all seemed right with the world.

Jason and I looked at each other, immediately thought it best to move on without dwelling on the highly sensitive subject of student IEPs, but knowing that what we had witnessed was no small feat. We had created an environment where special ed and English teachers coexisted seamlessly, and special ed and mainstream students sat side by side without feeling patronized or singled out. That, to us, meant as much as any test score could ever mean.

So it made perfect sense that, at the close of our eighth year, administration decided that it would be in everyone's best interest if Jason and I no longer taught together. Repeated requests to the director of special education to explain the move were met with a refrain of "Change is good." Sometimes, if she really felt like elaborating, she might add, "Think of this as an opportunity."

Jason was asked what he would prefer to teach since he was being moved out of English.

"I've been teaching math for awhile," he responded to the question about his preferences. "I'd be happy to keep doing that or social studies. Just not science. Please, anything but Earth science."

"Okay," the director told him. "That shouldn't be a problem."

Through either small group alternative classes of his own or as a mainstream co-teacher, Jason now teaches Earth science all day. Every day. For the entire year. The guy just can't catch a break.

Meanwhile, I endure student after student stopping in the room, noticing only one teacher desk, and asking incredulously about Jason's reassignment. I repeat myself every time to the set of questions that sounds amazingly similar, responding with, "We've been split up. . . . He's teaching science now. . . . Yes, science. . . . How is it without him? It sucks. . . . I don't know why. . . . That's just the way it is. . . ."

Sadly, I'm telling the truth. I don't know why. It simply is. Our academic leaders in the administration rarely see fit to offer explanations for their decisions. If we're kept in the dark about the decision-making process, maybe we'll be less critical. At the very least, they won't have to look any of us in the eye when they make drastic moves. Better to seem arbitrary, which is frustrating but not really arguable, than make a deliberate move with logic that can be called into question and countered. This mentality plays out repeatedly, perhaps best illustrated by the decision to shuffle every department in the building for seemingly no reason. Classrooms were all packed and moved at no small expense (hundreds of moving boxes were purchased, dozens of staffers were paid to spend the summer moving boxes and furniture from one floor to another, one wing to another). Every request for an explanation was met with the terse, ambiguous response of, "It makes the most sense."

Maybe that's why I'm so grateful for the companionship of colleagues like Jason, who I can count more as a friend than a coworker. The administration isn't going to make life any easier for us, so we may as well at least have each other to make life more bearable. I believe in business that would be referred to as having a horizontal support network with little vertical backing.

I may be wrong, but I guess that's one more reason I'm not in business. I'll stay in the classroom looking at the empty space where Jason's desk sat for years, thinking about the importance of companionship, all the places it got us, and how I wish more teachers could experience what we had.

CHAPTER 20

Curtain Call

I T TOOK SEVERAL YEARS to master the art and craft of working
with my students, as opposed to against them, for them, or in spite
of them. Once I got past the initial ineptitude of inexperience and
through the depression of disillusionment, I actually became a fairly
effective teacher. As already mentioned, the decision to commit to an
extended stay at my current school after such a tenuous start lent a new
outlook to my daily routine. Life was, I daresay, pretty good. I even had
a summer draw to a close without any sense of dread about what a new
school year would bring.

Of course, something that good couldn't last.

Even at my best as a teacher, I was better still as a theater director. Both when heading up direction of a show or serving as technical
director on a production, I was good at my job. Students responded to
my guidance, opportunities to stretch my creativity abounded, and I
managed to provide new and unique experiences for cast, crew, and
audiences alike. While I saw myself excelling in my duties, I would

eventually come to realize I was not pleasing everyone. I am, I think it's safe to say, a type B personality through and through. The theater department I had been so proud to be involved in was run for many years by a man who is, I think it's equally safe to say, a type A personality through and through.

After adapting to the expectations of being a technical director in a high-caliber program, head directing opportunities came my way. It became even more apparent that my strengths and weaknesses were a perfectly contrasting complement to my older colleague Bil. We were the yin and yang theater-department directors, I thought. An odd couple that somehow managed to work. At a glance, we seemed similar. We were both over six feet tall, prone to varying degrees of facial hair, and rarely seen in anything other than jeans. That's about where the similarities ended. Whereas I tend to be too quiet in conversation, Bil was always uncomfortably loud. I would take time to develop concepts around a central image or theme, picture an entire set in my head, and then lead the tech crew in building each component by sketching out on scraps of paper and lumber at hand. Bil was a planner. He was all about lists, grids, and sublists. If I could be equated with a surrealist painting, Bil was an architectural blueprint—both of us valuable for our individual strengths but not something you'd typically find displayed side by side. Usually people seek out one or the other depending on their needs, not both.

Even though we got along well, it was clear from the beginning that I tried Bil's patience. He would come to my classroom to run some ideas past me for a play and instead shake his head.

"Look at this mess," he would boom in that deep bass smoker's voice. "This is terrible. How do you expect kids to learn in here?"

"What?" I would ask innocently, knowing exactly to what he was referring. My desk was a shapeless blob of papers, folders, and brochures. Separate piles, the limit of my daily organizational skills, had morphed into a single heap.

"What kind of example are you setting here?"

"I can find anything I need," I argued. I would then pull something out of the mound and say, "See, I knew right where this was." That would usually be enough to keep him from getting too specific or personal in his disapproval of how I conduct myself. Then Bil found it impossible to bite his tongue any longer.

I pride myself on being fairly self-aware and ready to acknowledge my faults, but I was completely unprepared for the snowballing barrage of complaints, criticisms, and (eventually) actual verbal attacks that would follow over the next couple of years. My overworked, disorganized, always-behind-schedule tendencies that I have already described had reached a breaking point with Bil, and he minced no words in telling me so. I was devastated.

Theater had consumed countless hours. It had been the source of some of my greatest feelings of accomplishment in my adult life. The working relationship I had with my techies and actors were, I was sure, what kept me in the teaching profession through low points. When the stress of a dress rehearsal gone wrong got too overwhelming, any little problem could make Bil an absolute bear. Just as he began to be more prone to aggressively calling me out on any act or decision or flaw he found unacceptable, I distanced myself from him whenever possible. Any semblance of friendship was simply a coworker arrangement. I made conscious efforts to avoid him when possible.

The proverbial straw that broke the camel's back came one December in the early steps of producing a horrific staging of Disney's cash cow bubblegum excuse for musical theater, a show so devoid of originality it was simply titled *High School Musical*. Bil chose a show with no artistic merit simply because he wanted to tap into the popular buzz of the movie. Preteen girls from the middle school up the hill would ensure sellout performances. In my mind, after Bil so frequently insisted on choosing plays and musicals based on the value of what students would learn from the experience of staging them, any performance of this play would be a sellout performance regardless of audience size.

In classic fashion, Bil crafted numerous grids and charts listing every scene, complete with songs, page numbers, locations, etc. He handed me a script, a chart, and said, "Let me know when you have a design."

I struggled with this one more than any show before it. The list called for things like 30 student desks. Bil would be staging action around the furniture in the scene, and our choreographer would be planning the dance to fit around and on the furniture of the scene, yet I was supposed to blindly place items with no idea about whether or not it fit their ideas or needs. I asked the choreographer what she preferred for desk placement. She diplomatically said she could work around anything as long as I got her a floor plan soon, while she was still developing the choreography. I asked Bil what he preferred for desk placement, and he told me he wasn't about to do my job for me. He had too much work of his own to spend any time doing mine for me.

So I struggled to place little pieces of props and furniture on a couple dozen maps of the stage so he could tell performers where to stand and the choreographer could finish her, well, choreography. I had just finished directing a show for which Bil did my set, and his efforts involved little more than a couple of platforms a few inches off the floor. What furniture and other props I wanted to use were decisions left totally to me. Apparently Bil thought I should do for him what he was not willing to do for me. No one would give me answers, I felt like I was taking stabs in the dark developing plans for a show (and director) I had little respect for, and as special icing on the cake, a nasty stomach virus had me out of commission for a few days. Even without getting sick, though, I clearly wasn't going to meet the deadline for the floor plans.

When I returned from my sick days, I had a stern email waiting for me explaining that my failure to adhere to deadlines was having an adverse effect on the other aspects of the production. I replied with my usual apologies and promises to get it done soon, but I again mentioned my frustration over the lack of guidance or ideas about where everything ought to be.

If there's one thing I've learned as a passive-aggressive introvert with an aptitude for written language, it's that I can rely a little too much on email. When Bil responded, he wasted no time telling me that I had done enough shows here to know my job and what I was expected to do.

Then came my mistake. In an effort to both lighten the mood and let Bil know I didn't care for the way he was handling this, I sent a message stating, "I can't help but feel like I'm being scolded here." He lit into me once again. I *was* being scolded, he wrote, because I was in the midst of dropping the ball in a monumental fashion and making everyone suffer because of it, especially him. When that message came in at the end of the school day, I took the uncharacteristic steps (literally and figuratively) of walking directly to Bil's room to hash this out face-to-face.

As soon as I showed up and clearly wanted to take issue with his description of the job I was doing, Bil belittled me in his classroom so loudly that passersby in the hall and teachers in the next rooms wondered if security needed to be called in. Most of the exact words are now a blur, but key exchanges stand out vividly. As I reassured Bil repeatedly that I would get the job done, he stated that wasn't enough.

"I know you'll get it done. You always do, but you drive me crazy in the process."

"I'm sorry. I thought you'd want something that made more sense than me making guesses at what you might want, but I'll just make the plans," I replied.

"That's not good enough. You always do this. I've had it."

"I said I'm sorry. I said I'll take care of it. What more do you want me to say?" That opened the door for the answer I wasn't prepared to hear.

"I want you to go think about your future with this program."

I was stunned, speechless. He continued.

"Go think about what you're doing to all of us. You're careless, unprofessional, and you're dragging us down. You're a terrible role model for the kids. I want you to seriously rethink your involvement in theater here."

That humiliation—the sting of that lashing—is an experience I will never forget or forgive. Listening to the man I had for years seen as a friend and inspirational mentor of sorts tell me I was a terrible role model to my students and a detriment to the theater program I had devoted myself to irreparably shook what had been an utterly consistent source of personal fulfillment. Even at my most exhausted, my most frustrated, my most angry points in a production, part of me was always relieved to be actively pursuing my creative passion for the theater. Bil opened my eyes to many of my shortcomings that I had been previously unwilling or unable to see in their entirety, but he did it in a way that made me retreat instead of move forward. The thought of working on a play began to make me feel sick instead of excited. I immediately wondered if I could finish the show, let alone complete the obligation I had signed on for with the upcoming winter play. In all my time since arriving here, there had been only two shows I was not directly involved in.

A couple of years after beginning at my school, there was a production I just couldn't handle anymore. *OnStage*, as it was called, was a song-and-dance revue, with the selections, theme, and some sort of unifying structure coming from the head director. This was the one show of the year not directed by Bil or me, but instead it was the creative brainchild of the head choir director. After a few years of working nonstop productions all year and a couple of attempts at *OnStage*, I decided that the ambiguity of the director's expectations, mixed with an outsider designing the set plans, combined with a ridiculously tight time frame, to be too taxing. The following year I sat out that show. The next year, I sat it out again. I watched as a new technical director took over and ran through the same mix of successes and failures I had endured when I began. I became concerned, though, when I perceived more failures than successes and worried about my tech kids I was still so devoted to the rest of the year. After some soul-searching, some talks with the choir director, and a healthy dose of financial need, I returned to work on *OnStage*.

The time off had done me good, and taking over the set design responsibilities eliminated the extra layer of complication the previous productions had. I was back to doing every show of the year, busier than ever, and thrilled to again be such an active and integral element of our program. That's why it pained me to contemplate cutting back again when the working relationship with Bil turned so sour. One explosion led to another, and I began to swear I would never do tech for him again as he would swear he'd never hire me to do tech again.

The next year I started the school year directing a play, working tech for *OnStage*, and then sitting back to watch one of my former students, a stellar technician, take over my job as tech director for Bil's shows. I was no longer integral, no longer woven inseparably into the theater season. This is the same crossroads school year that ended my teaching partnership with Jason. So much for feeling good about my job, feeling like I had a handle on everything, and the noteworthy absence of dread whenever returning to school from a break. The dread was back in a big way.

Many of the same old questions returned to haunt me. What kept sabotaging me any time I felt good about myself professionally? I had dismissed myself as a hopeless malcontent only to wonder again if I was placing way too much weight on the need to be happy at work. Is happiness really something a person can strive for professionally? What would an interviewer say if I listed happiness among my career objectives? Yet I felt myself yearning for that elusive happiness, and so I cut myself loose. Like a climber dangling from a lifeline that threatens to pull other climbers off the cliff, I cut the rope that bound me to the theater program. I would no longer work any show in any capacity. I simply needed out. Happiness was no longer to be found in my beloved theater as long as Bil was around and asserted authority over me using a previously unknown job title of Director of Theater to express his disdain for my work on shows he wasn't even involved in.

I cursed myself for voluntarily giving up something that had been so important to me for so long, and then I blamed Bil for driving me out. In one breath I would wonder how I could be so unprofessional as to consistently miss deadlines or lose receipts for departmental purchases before switching to wondering how Bil could be so unprofessional as to yell at a fellow teacher like I was some neighborhood stray dog shitting on his lawn.

Once again, teaching seemed to be nothing more than a balancing act between the greatest rewards a job can offer and the infuriating byproducts of egos, confusion, tension, and all the other crap that blurs the line between high school kids and high school staff.

This is the moment I find myself navigating as I write this book. Maybe it finally is time to get out, or maybe all the other distractions will finally fade to the point where I can really excel as a teacher—just a teacher. Maybe this is just one more valley to wait out until everything inevitably improves, even if only temporarily.

In any case, I hacked Bil and his cancer from my side. In my haste I may have left a scar, but the prognosis is good.

CHAPTER 21

Blurring the Divide

T HE ASSISTANT PRINCIPAL AT ST. FRANCIS HIGH SCHOOL once pulled me into his office and gave me a stern warning. I needed to do anything within my power to remind students of the distinct line between them and me. They were students, I was a teacher, and there was supposed to be some sort of minefield between us as a buffer zone. His concern stemmed from a handful of kids who knew me the year before when I was brought on board to direct a one-act play. I was still in college and hadn't put much thought into what they should call me, so out of habit I told them to call me Nathan. The next fall, when I joined the faculty full time, one or two of the kids who were still around from the previous year's production continued to call me Nathan. To this day I still don't know who, but someone overheard it and ran to the AP's office to complain. And so I sat in his office, not quite in trouble but not quite off the hook.

That was when I first started to give up shaving. There wasn't much to be done about my age. I was only about five years older than some of the seniors, so physically I was going to look pretty similar. Fortunately I was substantially taller than most of them, but I needed more. What started out previously as a purely symbolic move—not shaving during final exam week so my outward disheveled appearance matched my exhausted state of mind—turned into a tool to try and create the separation the administration wanted to me to maintain from my students. General scruff evolved into a goatee, which in turn grew into some sort of bizarre King Tut extension of my chin. I gradually got a little better at keeping myself from looking completely ridiculous, but the basic habits took hold. From that point onward I would be, oh, let's say *inconsistent* when it came to that aspect of my grooming. Even now, when there's no mistaking I'm quite a bit older than any of my students, I meander from full beard to goatee to stubble.

And, as I creep up on the ripe old age of 33, I find myself increasingly less concerned about maintaining artificially formal distances from students. I maintain professional boundaries, don't get me wrong, but I'm happy to head out for appetizers with a couple of recent grads home from college. I'm happy to bullshit with kids in the morning before school starts. I may even take on a role that I can't quite identify. Not a parent, not one of their peers, but something in-between. An uncle, perhaps? That's a role I'm used to.

For my birthday recently, a dozen or so students—mostly techies led by a crazy Canadian—got into my classroom the night before and decorated it with crepe paper and balloons, complete with a Superman piñata hanging in the center of the room. After school that day they met down the hall before beginning a kazoo processional to my room. Earlier that same year, well aware of my fondness for coffee—insatiable addiction, really—they gave me a Caribou Coffee world coffee tour subscription as a Christmas gift. For each of the next six months I received two pounds of coffee from various coffee-bean-growing regions of the world. Again spearheaded by Canuck, the card—signed by all who contributed—amazingly included not only numerous current students, but a number of alumni as well.

That first year in St. Francis I would have been terrified that some other teacher or the assistant principal would walk in on scenes such as that over-the-top birthday party and scold me. Clearly I was way too familiar with my students if they felt at liberty to throw me a party. Now I just don't care what any of them have to say. I'm comfortable with the boundaries as I've set them. I refuse to hear about risky behavior on their parts, including drugs, drinking, and sex. Despite numerous invitations, including from parents, I have never attended a cast party after a performance. I've hired students as babysitters or to aid with manual labor in the yard, but to me that's no different than anyone hiring a couple of high school kids from the neighborhood. For my part, I will be more frank with the students I know well about what I'm doing and why, such as why I chose a certain play to direct and how I came up with the casting decisions, or what I was thinking when I gave a certain assignment.

Kim sometimes teases me a little about how close I can become with some of my students, particularly the tech kids and especially after they graduate. "They love you," she'll say. "And you love that they love you."

True, there's a little vanity involved in being at the receiving end of their kind words and generosity, but the truth of the matter is that I simply like them. A handful of current students and countless former students would really make for better friends than the majority of the teachers on staff.

Kim also can't help but shake her head when she walks by and sees me once again on Facebook, checking in with any number of current or former students.

"Quit stalking them," she'll say.

"I'm not stalking—just keeping in touch."

"You're going to turn into one of those people who only have virtual friends online."

"No I won't," is my brilliant retort before adding, "I just got a couple of messages I need to reply to, that's all."

"Uh-huh. Let me know when you're done catching up on your gossip."

She may have a point. Some of what I come across on Facebook is a little juvenile, but for the most part I relish the connection I am able to maintain with so many grads. Most of us teachers see seniors walk out the door at the end of high school, never to be seen or heard from again. Updates are passed along second- or thirdhand as lounge conversation over lunch one day, and that's it. I'm actually able to hear firsthand how college is going, how high school did or didn't prepare them, and what changes have been made in the college major or career plans they thought they had when they left my classes. One of my colleagues recently mentioned how some of her students had tracked down a former student teacher on Facebook and conversed with her briefly online.

"Seems awfully unprofessional to me," she muttered in disgust. "I can't imagine anyone thinking it's a good idea to be on Facebook with students."

"Well . . ." I started to respond, but I just didn't know how to defend myself on the spot. I wasn't prepared to spontaneously articulate the value of the Facebook connections like I have here just now. "Well," I started again, "I don't think that it's *all* bad."

"Maybe not," she huffed, "but you'll never catch me on there."

True, I doubted I would ever catch her on Facebook, largely because I doubted she'd have anyone to network with. I did have people to connect with, though, and it became a source of satisfaction. After all, how many teachers would you choose to add to your list of friends? The sense of not just acceptance but actual approval that accompanied each "friend request" provided that rare feedback I wished for so often. I might not be so bad at this after all if so many students wouldn't mind keeping in touch.

In honest reflection, I think I feel a need to defend being a Facebook friend or a pseudo-uncle because I know this does not automatically translate to being a good teacher. A birthday party might affirm I was liked, but what of the job I was doing providing an education? How sad it seems that even simple sources of joy still raise insecurity over my effectiveness. It's gratifying to build these relationships, but what of the actual teaching? Do my students ever learn? Maybe I just need to relax and gain a little self-confidence. Problem is, whenever I see reason to feel confident and competent, I focus on everything that belittles my successes. Once again a self-sabotaging malcontent, it seems. The answers to it all must lie somewhere at the beginning.

CHAPTER 22

Open Letter Number 5

D EAR NEW TEACHERS,

I never thought I would supervise a student teacher, but I always thought I'd be good at it. I would, it's safe to say, both model effective teaching *and* demonstrate all sorts of things teachers ought not do. I considered myself at the perfect point in my career for such a responsibility. I had been at it long enough that I managed to figure out a thing or two about surviving this line of work, yet I still had vivid memories of the monumental disconnect between being a student in a class and becoming the teacher of a class. The lifelong vets, as good as their intentions may be, simply don't have that fresh clarity to draw from.

One fall, as a new year began, a colleague in the English department struggled with a student teacher that left us all baffled. It seemed a teacher, someone who inherently must work with dozens of people face-to-face on a daily basis, probably should enjoy working with people. A willingness to speak comes in handy. Bathing on occasion is useful too. With this nightmare supervising assignment underway, no one else seemed too eager to volunteer when word spread of another student teacher arriving for the second half of the year in need of a cooperating/supervising teacher. I thought the odds of the next student teacher being a dramatic improvement were in my favor, so I gladly volunteered. I have such a hard time taking myself seriously that I doubted those in charge of things like student teacher assignments would ever look my way. When the placement was formally assigned and I started to plan for weeks of serving as a mentor teacher, my days took on a new light.

I saw myself differently when I knew I would assist someone entering the profession. I wondered from time to time if I should be doing more to take myself seriously. I caught myself reflecting on my work in ways I hadn't for a long time. As long as I could remember, I dwelled on the negative, beat myself up for my weaknesses, and wished things were magically different.

Once again, I was wrong. I did not make a good mentor for a student teacher. I am too cynical, too *laissez-faire,* too unorganized to foster professional growth in a student teacher. The young woman who came into my classroom to teach was polite enough to humor my self-described pearls of wisdom. She wondered, when I shared with her all these moments I'm not so proud of, what exactly I was trying to tell her. My effort to seem as authentic, honest, and fallible as possible only served to diminish how much stock she put in anything I had to say. Indeed, many people wonder how much stock to put into anything I have to say. And so I return to the realm of everyday teacher, probably never to return to the realm of student teacher supervisor.

Even still, I would like to take a moment to speak to those of you about to enter the profession. I do not profess to be some sort of know-it-all expert or exemplar of fabulous teaching—I think all of the preceding chapters have quashed any possibility of giving that impression—but I do have some things to say. You see, I started writing this book out of urgent uncertainty. I needed to try and figure out this damned teaching thing. Teaching was becoming my identity, and I didn't know how to feel about that. Conflicted emotions abounded: I scoffed at being told teaching was a noble calling while wishing with the same breath I could earn more respect. I lamented the salary and then counted my blessings for being able to provide for my family. A local newspaper reporter who once wrote a story about the experience of substitute teaching for a week had something along these lines to say: Teaching is too hard for those who don't care, and too hard on those who do. I again felt like a cog in a system of futility where no one grew or learned, but I refused to completely abandon my hope of someday serving as an inspiration for somebody.

Frequently I find that when students are struggling to understand something, whether it's Shakespeare or dependent clauses, simply talking them through what they do understand can be just enough to lead to illumination. Just so, I feel as though I have talked my way through the little bit I did know with certainty about my job only to discover some deeper truths I never saw before.

I have used several words to describe the angst I felt . . . discontent, hollowness, apathy, futility, ambivalence . . . and I finally feel equipped to identify the source of it all. People go into the teaching profession with good motives. None of the burned-out teachers I know became a teacher with the goal of becoming the empty shell of an educator they eventually became. They became teachers for powerful, deeply personal reasons. Maybe they saw pure joy in a young child's curiosity about the world. Maybe there were inspirational teachers along the way. Maybe they held a deep passion for some subject area and wanted to share the enthusiasm with classes of their own.

Whatever drove any teacher to this career, it was not out of greed, ambition, or a lust for fame (see my earlier comments about getting hollered at in parking lots). And not all of them are burned-out. There are thousands across the nation just like us: anywhere from first-year newbie to 40-year veteran, all wondering about the same questions and dilemmas I have raised. There is, oddly, some comfort in that. Here we are, all adrift together. Teaching can be such an isolated experience that, at times, it helps to remember that. You're not inadequate; we all are.

While people were drawn into teaching by some intangible force in their core, the sad reality is that teachers rarely ever feel like successes. This, future teachers, is the epiphany I had while writing this book that I had to share with you. Not to discourage you, but to try and preempt later disappointment. It took me eight years to realize I was feeling unfulfilled—like a failure—all because I had no realistic way to feel fulfilled, content, and successful. That is, everything I thought I knew about what makes a good teacher turned out to be minor in the larger scope of what all teachers can and should do for students.

Personal satisfaction doesn't come from anything that can be tested or quantified. Contentment can't be found in No Child Left Behind. Carefully typed lesson plans do not alleviate frustrations over the incompetence of principals and administrators. In fact, many of the things that I used to think mattered most about teaching— meaningful assignments and activities, effective discipline, and thorough feedback and grading—now matter little to me. Well, they still matter as much as they ever did, but I don't beat myself up for coming up short in these areas now.

If a final reckoning of my career thus far were to be held today, and all my successes and failures were tallied and ranked, the compelling reality is that the most important things I have ever done as a teacher have nothing to do with any of the classes I have taught. The things that matter most are the encounters, however fleeting or prolonged, with individual students that actually shaped their lives. It took years to start to hear from students that I mattered, but when good kids with good hearts were kind enough to tell me I helped them, I inspired them, or I made their day a little better, it all became clear. The nasty political rhetoric about accountability, standards, and merit didn't twist daggers in my side anymore, because I knew something the politicians still don't know. They can't pin me down. My effectiveness is not going to show up on a test or reveal itself during a classroom observation. It shows up when a girl writes after graduating years ago to tell me she contemplated suicide before I was the first person to express concern over her well-being, and I saved her life. It shows up when a mother stops me to say that her son has never liked English before now, and it warms her heart to see him excited about a core academic subject.

As I mentioned, though, teachers rarely get these opportunities to feel like successes. As rejuvenating as such emails from former students and comments from parents can be, they are too few and too irregular to combat all the drudgery and absurdity of the job. The classroom is full of students and teachers consumed with the here and now. It takes quite a leap of faith for a teacher to believe that efforts that seem futile today will pay dividends down the road, but such faith in the future is the only antidote I have for the inevitable despair I felt when looking for instant gratification as a good teacher. It was especially frustrating because, after the school day was done, my work with the theater did provide that instant gratification. I saw the immediate fruits of my efforts when working on a show with techies or actors, but concrete progress in a classroom is much harder to spot, measure, and appreciate.

Academic success takes a leap of faith, as well. A typical kid, starting with half-day kindergarten through his or her senior year of high school, spends about 15,300 hours in school. That's out of the 113,880 hours they lived over those same 13 years. This means a student's entire public school education will have occupied about 13.5 percent of his or her life during that time. Of that fraction spent in school, my cut for a kid I have in class all year is about 150 hours. The knowledge I am to impart on my students is to be done in .0009 percent of their time in school. I don't point this out because I'm a sucker for numbers or to lower expectations about what I can accomplish in my classes. This simply needs to be stated, acknowledged, and remembered any time any teacher in any school feels like a failure.

None of us is perfect, and there is not one among us who has managed to avoid mistakes in their career. Indeed, mistakes are a regular occurrence. If a teacher can't spot the mistakes, they lack the humility, concern, and self-awareness the job demands. It works out, though. In the end, kids become adults. Many of those broken kids heal. Except for those among us who end up irreparably fried and jaded, we live to teach another day.

And so, new teachers, embrace feeling like a failure with gusto. Accept that your success—your effectiveness—is a slippery sensation that is nearly impossible to accomplish deliberately but sneaks up as a pleasant surprise when least expected. Asking for anything more than that will at best cause frustration; at worst it will leave you bitter and calloused beyond any resemblance to the hopeful new teacher in the mirror today.

CHAPTER 23

Crystal Ball

S OME CHOOSE TO DISMISS THE FUTURE as an inevitable
surprise that will reveal itself to us when the time is right. Others
make their fortunes by telling us what's to come, feeding off our
culture's insatiable need to know as much as possible as quickly as
possible. I view the future as an endless source of daydream fodder.

Clearly there are some predictions I can make here that will be
little more than restating the obvious, such as the undoubted merge
that will continue to take place between classroom experiences and
online experiences. It's also safe to say that regardless of what happens
to national initiatives like No Child Left Behind, our culture of testing as the first line of quality control won't be coming to an end any
time soon. What then, can I offer as an insider's take on what's coming
down the pike?

Choice will continue to be the bone of contention. I hope the
debate over vouchers for private school choice will fizzle, but other matters of choice will take on greater significance. Open enrollment, where
people can enroll to attend a school outside the district or attendance

area where they reside, will grow from the current issue surrounding athlete recruiting and turn into an issue of general student recruiting. Everything from test scores to desegregation to balancing special-education populations will become a matter of interdistrict cooperation or competition, depending on how it unfolds.

As far as special education is concerned, it is my fear that a backlash is brewing. After the years of fighting it took for protective rights to be put in place for students with special needs and disabilities, we could see some of the first decreases in rights and protections if funding and regulatory matters aren't addressed. The federal government, since first implementing the Individuals with Disabilities Education Act in 1975, has never once come close to providing the funds to cover 40 percent of the cost of putting the new protective regulations into practice. As states and districts divert money to fulfill the legal and moral obligations of providing quality education to *all* students, citizens who grow weary of general funding shortfalls look toward the large slice of the pie taken up by special education and wish they could find ways to tap into that money. As testing regulations break student bodies into demographic subgroups to close achievement gaps, incidents where schools fail to reach the highest possible governmental rating because of one test score within one special-education subgroup can have a demoralizing effect. Instead of a building's staff coming together in support of one another, a climate could develop where special-education staff are blamed for schools getting lower ratings, or, worse yet, special-education students themselves are viewed with disdain.

Finally, high schools are going to find themselves under increased pressure to provide practical career training. The days of operating under the assumption that every graduate is going on to a four-year college are gone. We now recognize that not every student's needs are met by following that path, and that community and technical colleges are another option worth promoting. We are also beginning to see advanced career-oriented course offerings available as electives in a variety of fields. The new elements I see coming on the horizon are comprehensive programs for career preparation, right down to specific English, social studies, science, and math courses being tailored to fit a student's chosen career track. This begins to smack of the European tracking model, but I don't see our schools adapting to that degree. Instead, I see this as a voluntary program spurred on by businesses looking for better prepared, earlier prepared employees.

As for that technology piece that will undoubtedly change the look and feel of education profoundly, the transformation is already underway. Students have more instantaneous access to information than ever before possible. They are also surrounded by more junk information and commercialism than ever before. Computers are added to buildings at a dizzying pace, yet they can't keep up with demand for access. It's only a matter of time before every student has a laptop for personal use. Many classes will become hybrids mixing traditional in-room experiences with online work. In some cases, this model may even be used to divide students into shifts to ease facility overcrowding issues. The primary roadblock to this hybrid model is the resistance many parents and community members would have to high school students running free during every school day. Even this roadblock, though, could be surmounted if people decide it's the proper route. Technical advances have already granted parents real-time access to teachers' grade books, their son or daughter's attendance and discipline information, and online bill-paying options for everything from lunch money to activity participation fees. As videoconferencing becomes a viable option for teacher-student interaction, it's quite possible that classes in general will become webcast performances. Whether parents want to break down those last barriers to independence by watching their kids in class, or absent kids want to keep up to date with what they're missing, teachers may soon find themselves wondering if the webcam indeed adds 10 pounds. Of course, in the Age of Accountability, classroom cameras could also be used for monitoring teacher behavior and performance. The possibilities to deprive everyone of their privacy and professional trust are endless.

Then there's the crystal ball I try to gaze into now and then for myself. I made it past the point where I might run out the door screaming, past the point where I think teaching is going to be the death of me, and even past the point where it seems entering the teaching profession was a mistake. Yet I can't see the future with any certainty at all. Just because I no longer feel the urge to run out screaming doesn't mean I might not walk out casually. Even though I no longer think teaching is going to kill me, there are plenty of days it makes me literally and figuratively sick.

My new outlook has worked wonders on my daily mood. I find happiness in the handful of kids who I can tell are paying attention, smiling, and even thinking about what I say. I have managed to separate my sense of worth as a teacher from the handful of kids who look at me in disdain, resentful of everything I ask them to do and every limitation I put on their chances to chat at will. Most days, by any traditional definition, I feel like a failure as a teacher. I now look at that as a good day. While I feel more at ease to speak my mind with each year I entrench myself deeper at my school, I am generally a more pleasant person to deal with these days. At first glance, my life as a teacher has never been better.

Even with its fluctuations, though, my general unease remains constantly present. The double-hit of the past year—losing the two aspects of my job I cherished the most—leaves me pondering those same old questions one more time. How long will I teach in a high school? How long will I stay at this particular high school? The difference between the questions nagging me today and the same questions posed when I first began this book: I can wait for the answers. My initial despair came from seeking answers to these monstrous, abstract questions. It was as if someone had all the information I sought but refused to tell me. I was angry with this imaginary person, even though it undoubtedly was an extension of myself. I knew all along I didn't have answers to my own questions, but then I felt like I was supposed to. Now I wait.

I wait to see what the future has in store for me, I wait to see the future of our schools, and I wait to see what another year's rotation of students will bring. One class sent on their way into the world, another making the trip from the middle school to my room.

As I look to the teachers around me, it seems obvious in hindsight that the healthiest teachers—not necessarily the happiest, but the most stable—have adopted similar mind-sets. Patience. Look for the miniscule triumphs. Go ahead and ask questions, but quit holding your breath waiting for enlightenment. The future is coming, and we will simply adapt—just as we always have.

CHAPTER 24

Fear the Light, Seek the Dark

THAT'S WHAT MY TECH KIDS HAVE PRINTED ON THE T-SHIRTS they designed. For whatever reason, my techies don't do well in the spotlight. They prefer the view from backstage. There's nothing quite like it—standing just outside the pool of light—basking in the ambient glow but still anonymous behind the curtain. I must admit it's a pretty fun place to be. Backstage you're in the know, you see the hidden mechanisms of performance, the figurative cogs and gears that drive a show, all of the near disasters the audience never perceives from their seats on the other side of the curtains.

People see the techie T-shirts and assume it's some kind of moody Goth message about making oneself as pale as possible by avoiding any and all sunlight. I understand it, though. It's not about imagining how cool it'd be if vampires really existed. It's about influence—shaping what others see and playing a vital role in others' successes. They catch hell if they screw up and go almost completely unnoticed if they do their job well. They labor like sled dogs and are just as loyal. Their efforts show up in small degrees: making sure scenery moves to an exact position, a telephone rings just loudly enough to be heard but not so loudly as to sound unnatural, and lights come up after the actors are in position rather than catching them scurrying in the dark. All of these seemingly menial jobs the techies in the dark take on during a show add up to make them the hidden power behind the throne. No glory, but in many ways they pull all the strings. They oftentimes ask aloud why they keep doing this to themselves, and yet they show up day after day. They find the inspiration they need from deep within themselves, satisfaction simply from a job well done, fulfillment from a challenge faced and conquered.

Yeah, I can see how a person could get into that.

Epilogue

PERHAPS SPRING IS NOT AS BIG OF A DEAL ELSEWHERE, where the climate is milder and changing seasons are not so drastic. Here in Minnesota, though, a restlessness sets in by the end of February that can only be settled by melting snow, sunnier evenings, and stepping outside without a jacket. The pent-up energy of the masses deprived of fresh air and natural light too long releases itself with violence to match the weather. March in Minnesota can bring anything from blizzards to tornadoes. Temperatures can fluctuate dozens of degrees within a day's time. Just so, students and teachers can find themselves either smiling without reason, a bounce in their step, or find themselves agitated and quick-tempered.

In schools, the emergence of spring is the light at the end of the bleak academic tunnel. A reminder that any unpleasantness from the last few months is not permanent, and closure is near. A flurry of retirement announcements remind us daily that people really can teach for twenty, thirty, even forty years. I receive these announcements and again find myself wondering if I can make it that long, and, if I did, wondering if that would be a source of pride or disappointment.

One week after winter trimester came to a close this past March, I fumbled to answer a cell phone call while racing to school minutes before classes began. It was my friend Jason checking to see where I was.

"Are you here yet?"

"No," I replied. "Running a little late as usual. What's up?"

"I didn't see you at the meeting this morning, so I thought I'd check to see where you were."

"What meeting?"

"Well," he hesitated, "there was an emergency meeting. I'll—I'll tell you about it when you get here."

I was grateful to be within a couple of minutes of the parking lot, because a drawn-out commute would have provoked relentless speculation. As I sat down at my desk and unpacked my bag, Jason walked in carrying a couple papers. He handed them to me without a word, and I saw one read something like, "Aiding Adolescents in Times of Grief." The other was the copy of a police department press release.

Few details were clear, but this much was certain: one of our students was dead, and another was in custody under suspicion of fatally stabbing the victim. The victim's name rang a bell, but the suspect's name was very familiar. He had been in my class all of his ninth grade year, and three years later had just finished a term in my senior creative writing course. Rumors run rampant in high school no matter what the subject, but an incident this dramatic carried intensity far beyond simple gossip. Students knew far more than staff instantly. Technology again accelerated the spread of conjecture to blazing speeds.

Throughout the morning there was talk of multiple stab wounds, the victim attempting to ride away on his bike before collapsing in a snowbank that had not yet yielded to the fledgling spring weather.

The fight took place at the attacker's house—off school grounds and after school was out for the day, but when both the victim and the suspect were students from our school, it was nearly impossible to find someone who didn't feel directly connected in some way to what was being dubbed the first homicide in the history of our city.

A rational thinker with a level head might point out that this was a teenage dispute that took the most unfortunate of turns, but nothing more. The emotional truth, though, is that an entire community had its innocence shaken. I personally had a terrible time trying to reconcile the quiet, smiling kid I knew with the reports of the ferocity needed to stab someone multiple times in the back and abdomen with a kitchen knife. The boy had a rough year as a freshman, disappearing for a couple of weeks for substance abuse treatment, before returning and finishing the year on a strong upward trend. A few years later I thought of him as a success story—not a success I could necessarily take credit for, but still an example of everything working out in the end.

Instead, he sits in a cell facing second-degree murder charges, wondering if the prosecutor will be successful in his efforts to try him as an adult.

Of course, this doesn't even begin to touch on the shock and loss felt by the victim's friends and family.

Introspectively, though, I can only speak to my own experience. My experience was that yet again it was impossible to know, to gauge, to predict what lay beneath the façades of my students. There simply was no way to resolve the dissonance of the boy I knew from my class and the suspect in custody reported to have committed such acts. My life would go on. I was not losing a son to violence, a brother to the penal system, but there was a small kernel of buried optimism that I was losing. As clearly established throughout this entire book, optimism does not come easily to me. It wasn't just me, though. Thirty-year classroom warrior veterans shook their heads, worried eyes bearing an expression blending disbelief and confusion.

I originally wanted to end on the positive note of learning to recognize triumphs despite how obscure they might be, but it never fails that a dozen classroom victories will be eclipsed by one nightmare. If there's one thing to be said about teaching, it's that anyone with half a wit of self-awareness can never get too sure of themselves—something will inevitably ground you, humble you, or possibly even paralyze you.

A week ago the principal sent out an email informing us that a local man was charged with blackmail and extortion. It seems he targeted over 20 teachers from two districts, including ours, and sent them letters demanding $1,000 cash or he would report the teacher for sexual misconduct. Every targeted teacher was a male involved in coaching or advising a sport or activity. To my knowledge, none of the threatened teachers paid up or ever faced investigation for false allegations, but the story could undoubtedly have ended in a different manner. Sexual misconduct by teachers is exceptionally rare, but in the instances when it does occur the betrayal of public trust gets the media all fired up. Even the accusation could taint a professional's career. As baseless as these threats proved to be, a teacher or coach could not possibly walk away from it without being shaken.

Perhaps that's part of the problem I continue to face, even though I thought I had reached a contented state—reconciliation with my role. I was a teacher, not just someone who taught. The problem though, as pointed out by the lovely thirty-nine-year-old man who lived with his parents just a little north of my home, was that it always seemed someone was targeting me. I didn't get one of his infamous letters, but it was one more illustrative case of a public on the attack. A real downside to constantly reminding myself of all my faults and limitations is that I have become extra sensitive to attacks. I am not the best I could be, and I am not half as good as many of my coworkers, so I simply begin to assume that every attack—every criticism—must be somehow directed at me.

Among many others, the crucial difference between me ten years ago and me today is that I can brush those nagging distractions aside. I can't get myself to ignore them completely; I'll still gnash my teeth now and then. I can shove them to the periphery, though.

Of course, every now and then I like to pull those distractions back from the periphery and study them for a bit in writing. The creation and subsequent publishing of this book has been an odyssey unto itself, and I often get stopped by family members, friends, even chance acquaintances, and am asked to describe and explain what the book is about. I know they are well-intentioned and kind to have any interest at all, but I still hesitate for a second before responding. Mentally I ponder if this person really wants a thorough explanation or a dust jacket summary.

"It's about teaching," I tell them with a keen eye on their reaction to see if they want more specifics than that. The specifics are a bit tricky to pin down.

"Oh," they respond, thinking out loud. "So is it... is it a textbook for teachers?"

"No, no, no." There is a fine line of laughter—a line between laughing at the thought of me writing a how-to book on teaching and laughing mockingly at them for asking in the first place. "No, it's not a textbook, unless people want to read about what not to do."

"Oh, so it's . . . Well, what is it about then?"

"It's all about what a sorry excuse for a teacher I am and all the reasons I shouldn't be doing this."

"Really?" Some people at this point get my sense of humor. Others wonder why a seemingly rational person would publish a laundry list of reasons to be fired.

"Well, that may be stretching it a little."

Truth is, there were times when I felt I was laying out the case against me, almost as if I were trying to convince myself that I was a failure. Ultimately it boils down to an exploration of self-doubt in an effort to reemerge more confident, more aware, and more comfortable in my own skin. I am fallible, I will tell you about my weaknesses all day long, and I may even joke about what a terrible teacher I am. Call me a terrible teacher, though, and I will lash out at you. One more of my inconsistencies, I guess.

Commiserating is therapeutic. Some unique, personal experiences are surprisingly universal. I mentioned early on that despite the highly social nature of this profession, it often feels like lonely work. I was adrift, coughing and gagging as I flailed to keep my head above water, friends and coworkers throwing lifelines all around me, but I had to swim to safety on my own. One thing I noticed while adrift was how many others were bobbing in the water just as I was. I hope they have people throwing them lifelines, even if they need to swim for themselves. However they get there, it can only help to know that it is possible—you can stay in survival mode for years and still pull through.

The turnover rate for teachers in the first few years of employment is insane. Maybe it separates the wheat from the chaff, so to speak, but a good many of us make it through those first few years only to wonder if we should have been weeded out. I wondered about that, wrote down my thoughts to try and find the answer, and ended up content to decide there doesn't have to be an answer. I can work at helping kids any way I can, with everything from Shakespeare to abusive homes, without knowing if I should have been fired four years ago or will quit four years from now.

I take the dissonance I feel as a good sign. If I still see the good in that smiling, quiet boy from my creative writing class instead of only seeing a violent felon, I may make it another 30 years. It's certainly a good place to start.

Reading Guide Questions

To whom is Miller addressing his book? Fellow teachers, parents, anyone who's in or has graduated from public school? What does Miller hope to accomplish with his book?

At the beginning of his book, Miller mentions a shop teacher telling him that teaching used to be much better. Miller says he doesn't want to dream about the good old days that probably never were, but he does indicate that the past had some advantages, notably fewer behavioral disorders among the students. What are some other things Miller mentions about teaching in the past?

What exactly does Miller see as the biggest difficulties in his job? Is it the threatening or disruptive students? Is it his heavy workload?

On page 7, Miller says, "all schools are pretty much equal: they are all full of broken kids." What, in Miller's opinion, is a broken kid?

While Miller clearly wants to help the "broken" students of his school, his experiences with the troubled boy James indicates that he has his limits as a counselor. Are his efforts helpful, or will his good intentions lead to problems?

In chapters 7 and 19, Miller criticizes school administrators. What kinds of obstacles do they put up for teachers, according to Miller?

On pages 42–43, Miller criticizes standardized testing as a way of improving the educational system and making sure students are learning. What are his arguments against standardized testing?

Miller acknowledges from the start of his book that something is wrong with schools, yet he doesn't think that standardized testing is useful, even when test scores indicate problems. What does he see as the difference between problems revealed by test scores and actual, real problems?

In chapter 5, Miller recalls a confrontation with a boy who threatened him. He mentions, as an example of lax discipline, that students can skip detention without repercussion. Does he suggest that discipline is part of the larger problem at his school?

How does Miller resolve his confrontation with the boys who threatened him? Does he act properly, or would there have been a better way to handle this particular problem?

At Miller's school, how serious and widespread is tension between ethnic groups? Why does he see the administration's solution—appointing a "diversity coordinator"—as effective? What does Miller do about this problem, and what are the signs that his method does or doesn't have an effect?

In chapter 12, Miller describes a "respect retreat," which is at least temporarily effective. But he notes that the students return to their old habits within days. Why didn't the lessons of the respect retreat have a more lasting impact?

Julie, a student described in chapter 13, presented huge challenges for Miller, and she was obviously a student with extreme problems, explained in part by her background. Did Miller make an effort to help Julie with her problems? Was he angry at himself for anything he tried or didn't try to do? What are other ways he could have handled Julie's disruptions and disregard for his teaching?

In chapter 15 (and in chapter 21), Miller describes the playful and silly things he frequently does in his classes. He argues that such seemingly frivolous actions may have educational benefits, but he also realizes that being silly may not be the best way to go about teaching. Are his arguments in favor of his frivolity plausible? Does he convince himself with his arguments, or does he want to be a different kind of teacher? Are there examples of his playfulness in other chapters?

In chapter 17, Miller lists the categories of students—A-ADHD, Quiet but Adjusted, Beautiful Witches, etc. Why does Miller put students in these categories? Are they even accurate? Would different or additional categories be more accurate?

In Open letter #4, addressed to parents, Miller doesn't blame parents for faults in the educational system as much as he warns them about the faults in administration, burned out teachers, and even teachers like himself. Does anything in the book indicate that Miller believes parents deserve a part of the blame for the problems in U. S. schools? Outside of his book, do Miller's experiences with the parents of his students match those of other teachers?

The topic of special ed students comes up in chapters 19 and 23. How was Miller able to achieve at least one significant success in teaching special ed students? Why does he predict that special education programs will cause problems in the future?

Throughout his book, Miller points out flaws in his own personality—the guilt he feels for not doing more for his students, his taking on more work than he can handle, his disorganization, his endless sarcasm. Does Miller's personality play a part in his problems with teaching and the educational system? If, for example, he could manage his time more effectively, would he be saying the same things about his job?

Miller ends his book with an example of one of the little triumphs that make his job bearable. According to him, looking for the minuscule triumphs is the only way teachers can keep a healthy attitude about their jobs. Are Miller's triumphs, as he sees them, worth celebrating, or does his parting message advocate a grasping at straws approach? And if someone were to suggest the latter to Miller, what do you think his response would be?

In chapter 9, Miller tells the reader about Gina and her difficulty with coming up with a topic for a research paper. Gina, according to Miller, is representative of a large group of high school students who don't see the value in working hard to excel in school. What has generated this attitude in so many students?

DATE DUE

MAR 2 5 2009

#47-0108 Peel Off Pressure Sensitive